MUSHROOMS
OF
IDAHO

IDENTIFICATION
RECORD BOOK

Hello Wild

Your Feedback is Appreciated!!!

Please consider leaving us "5 Stars" on your Amazon review.

Thank you!

Copyright © 2022 Hello Wild

All rights reserved.

This book or any portion thereof may not be reproduced or used in any manner whatsoever without the express written permission of the publisher except by reviewers, who may use brief quotations in a book review.

MUSHROOMS OF TEXAS

This Mushrooom Identification Record Book
Belongs To:

_____

There are thousands of species of mushrooms in the Gem State. With a climate that ranges from cold semi-arid, warm, humid continental, humid subtropical, hot, humid continental, subarctic, and hot summer mediterranean, a wide variety of mushrooms grow and thrive in the landscape. While many types are highly toxic, there are a number of edible mushrooms as well. Do not eat any mushroom without checking in person with a local, live mushroom expert.

Use this record book to identify and record the many types of mushrooms you come across!

Location

Site / GPS: _____ Date: _____

○ Living Tree ○ Leaf Litter ○ Mulch ○ Dead Tree or Wood ○ Grass
○ Soil ○ Other _____

Type of Tree(s) On or Near: _____

Forest Type: ○ Deciduous ○ Coniferous ○ Tropical ○ Other _____

Weather Conditions: _____

General

Size (overall height): _____ Color: _____ Spore Color: _____

Texture: ○ Tough ○ Brittle ○ Leathery ○ Woody ○ Soft ○ Slimy
○ Spongy ○ Powdery ○ Waxy ○ Rubbery ○ Watery (Other) _____

Bruising When Touched? ○ Yes ○ No   Notes: _____

Structures: ○ Cup ○ Ring ○ Warts

Cap Characteristics

Campanulate (bell-shaped)

Conical (triangular)

Cylindrical (shaped like half an egg)

Convex (outwardly rounded)

Flat (with top of uniform height)

Infundibuliform (deeply, depressed, funnel-shaped)

Depressed (with a low central region)

Umbonate (with a central bump or knob)

Surface Markings (warts, scales, slime, etc.): _____

Cap Margin: Smooth, Inrolled, Sinuous/Wavy, Other: _____

Color Changes: _____

Undercap

Gills ○
Attachment: Free or Decurrent
Spacing: Crowded, Close, Distant, Subdistant
Color/Bruising: _____

Pores ○
Color: _____
Pore Size: _____
Pore Pattern: _____

Teeth ○
Color: _____
Teeth Length: _____
Flesh: Soft or Tough

Gill Attachment

- **Free** (gills not attached to stem)
- **Adnexed** (gills attached narrowly to stem)
- **Sinuate** (gills smoothly notched and running briefly down stem)
- **Adnate** (gills widely attached widely to stem)
- **Descending** (gills running down stem for some length)

Stem Shape

   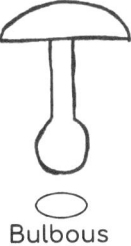 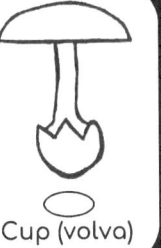

- Tapering
- Equal
- Club-Shaped
- Bulbous
- Cup (volva)

Common Mushrooms

Chanterelle
- Edible ☺
- Shape looks like bell of a trumpet
- Bright yellow/orange
- Similar look to Jack o'Lantern

Milk Mushroom
- Edible ☺
- Rounded caps that connect to an elongated, thick stem
- Smooth firm cap
- Color is pure white

Morels
- Edible ☺
- Honeycombed cap
- Most morels cap is longer than stem
- Spore print is usually light colored
- Interior is hollow

Porcini
- Edible ☺
- Large size
- Also known as king bolete
- Resembles reddish/brown hamburger bun

Shaggy Mane
- Edible ☺
- White shaggy cylindrical cap that turns black and inky with age
- Bell shape - mature
- Spore print is black

Death Cap
- Poisonous ☹
- Flattened top
- White cap with brownish scales
- Gills are free and white, turning green as they mature

False Morel
- Poisonous ☹
- Red-brown cap - irregularly lobed, like a brain
- Tube-like hollows
- Yellowish spore print
- Smooth with more wrinkles as it ages

Destroying Angel
- Poisonous ☹
- White stalk and gills
- White cap or white edge and yellowish, pinkish, or tan center
- Egg-shaped cap

Common Conecap
- Poisonous ☹
- Rust-colored brown gills and conical cap
- Surface smooth, dry
- Adnexed gills
- Slender straight stem
- Brown spore print

Deadly Galerina
- Poisonous ☹
- Brownish, sticky cap, yellowish to rusty gills, ring on stalk
- Edges are curved against gills
- Gills narrow, crowded

Lobster Mushroom
- Edible ☺
- Bumpy, reddish-orange exterior
- Fish-like taste
- Irregular shape with little to no stem
- Cracked cap

King Bolete
- Edible ☺
- Light brown to reddish brown
- Stem very thick and club shaped
- White closely spaced small pores
- White flesh

Spore Print

_____
_____
_____
_____
_____

Notes

Location

Site / GPS: _____ Date: _____

○ Living Tree ○ Leaf Litter ○ Mulch ○ Dead Tree or Wood ○ Grass
○ Soil ○ Other _____

Type of Tree(s) On or Near: _____

Forest Type: ○ Deciduous ○ Coniferous ○ Tropical ○ Other _____

Weather Conditions: _____

General

Size (overall height): _____ Color: _____ Spore Color: _____

Texture: ○ Tough ○ Brittle ○ Leathery ○ Woody ○ Soft ○ Slimy
○ Spongy ○ Powdery ○ Waxy ○ Rubbery ○ Watery (Other) _____

Bruising When Touched? ○ Yes ○ No Notes: _____

Structures: ○ Cup ○ Ring ○ Warts

Cap Characteristics

Campanulate (bell-shaped)

Conical (triangular)

Cylindrical (shaped like half an egg)

Convex (outwardly rounded)

Flat (with top of uniform height)

Infundibuliform (deeply, depressed, funnel-shaped)

Depressed (with a low central region)

Umbonate (with a central bump or knob)

Surface Markings (warts, scales, slime, etc.): _____

Cap Margin: Smooth, Inrolled, Sinuous/Wavy, Other: _____

Color Changes: _____

Undercap

Gills ○
Attachment: Free or Decurrent
Spacing: Crowded, Close, Distant, Subdistant
Color/Bruising: _____

Pores ○
Color: _____
Pore Size: _____
Pore Pattern: _____

Teeth ○
Color: _____
Teeth Length: _____
Flesh: Soft or Tough

Gill Attachment

○ Free
(gills not attached to stem)

○ Adnexed
(gills attached narrowly to stem)

○ Sinuate
(gills smoothly notched and running briefly down stem)

○ Adnate
(gills widely attached widely to stem)

○ Descending
(gills running down stem for some length)

Stem Shape

Tapering

Equal

Club-Shaped

Bulbous

Cup (volva)

Common Mushrooms

Chanterelle
- Edible ☺
- Shape looks like bell of a trumpet
- Bright yellow/orange
- Similar look to Jack o'Lantern

Milk Mushroom
- Edible ☺
- Rounded caps that connect to an elongated, thick stem
- Smooth firm cap
- Color is pure white

Morels
- Edible ☺
- Honeycombed cap
- Most morels cap is longer than stem
- Spore print is usually light colored
- Interior is hollow

Porcini
- Edible ☺
- Large size
- Also known as king bolete
- Resembles reddish/brown hamburger bun

Shaggy Mane
- Edible ☺
- White shaggy cylindrical cap that turns black and inky with age
- Bell shape - mature
- Spore print is black

Death Cap
- Poisonous ☹
- Flattened top
- White cap with brownish scales
- Gills are free and white, turning green as they mature

False Morel
- Poisonous ☹
- Red-brown cap - irregularly lobed, like a brain
- Tube-like hollows
- Yellowish spore print
- Smooth with more wrinkles as it ages

Destroying Angel
- Poisonous ☹
- White stalk and gills
- White cap or white edge and yellowish, pinkish, or tan center
- Egg-shaped cap

Common Conecap
- Poisonous ☹
- Rust-colored brown gills and conical cap
- Surface smooth, dry
- Adnexed gills
- Slender straight stem
- Brown spore print

Deadly Galerina
- Poisonous ☹
- Brownish, sticky cap, yellowish to rusty gills, ring on stalk
- Edges are curved against gills
- Gills narrow, crowded

Lobster Mushroom
- Edible ☺
- Bumpy, reddish-orange exterior
- Fish-like taste
- Irregular shape with little to no stem
- Cracked cap

King Bolete
- Edible ☺
- Light brown to reddish brown
- Stem very thick and club shaped
- White closely spaced small pores
- White flesh

Spore Print

Notes

_____
_____
_____
_____
_____
_____

Location

Site / GPS: _____ Date: _____

○ Living Tree ○ Leaf Litter ○ Mulch ○ Dead Tree or Wood ○ Grass
○ Soil ○ Other _____

Type of Tree(s) On or Near: _____

Forest Type: ○ Deciduous ○ Coniferous ○ Tropical ○ Other _____

Weather Conditions: _____

General

Size (overall height): _____ Color: _____ Spore Color: _____

Texture: ○ Tough ○ Brittle ○ Leathery ○ Woody ○ Soft ○ Slimy
○ Spongy ○ Powdery ○ Waxy ○ Rubbery ○ Watery (Other) _____

Bruising When Touched? ○ Yes ○ No   Notes: _____

Structures: ○ Cup ○ Ring ○ Warts   _____

Cap Characteristics

Campanulate (bell-shaped)

Conical (triangular)

Cylindrical (shaped like half an egg)

Convex (outwardly rounded)

Flat (with top of uniform height)

Infundibuliform (deeply, depressed, funnel-shaped)

Depressed (with a low central region)

Umbonate (with a central bump or knob)

Surface Markings (warts, scales, slime, etc.): _____

Cap Margin: Smooth, Inrolled, Sinuous/Wavy, Other: _____

Color Changes: _____

Undercap

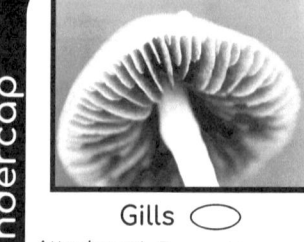

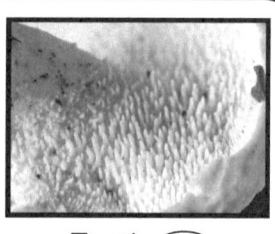

Gills ○
Attachment: Free or Decurrent
Spacing: Crowded, Close, Distant, Subdistant
Color/Bruising: _____

Pores ○
Color: _____
Pore Size: _____
Pore Pattern: _____

Teeth ○
Color: _____
Teeth Length: _____
Flesh: Soft or Tough

Gill Attachment

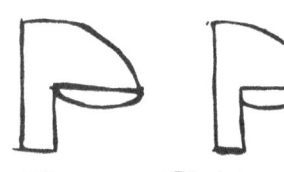

○ Free
(gills not attached to stem)

○ Adnexed
(gills attached narrowly to stem)

○ Sinuate
(gills smoothly notched and running briefly down stem)

○ Adnate
(gills widely attached widely to stem)

○ Descending
(gills running down stem for some length)

Stem Shape

    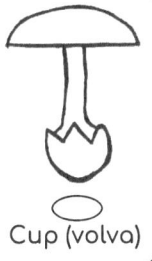

Tapering | Equal | Club-Shaped | Bulbous | Cup (volva)

Common Mushrooms

Chanterelle
- Edible ☺
- Shape looks like bell of a trumpet
- Bright yellow/orange
- Similar look to Jack o'Lantern

Milk Mushroom
- Edible ☺
- Rounded caps that connect to an elongated, thick stem
- Smooth firm cap
- Color is pure white

Morels
- Edible ☺
- Honeycombed cap
- Most morels cap is longer than stem
- Spore print is usually light colored
- Interior is hollow

Porcini
- Edible ☺
- Large size
- Also known as king bolete
- Resembles reddish/brown hamburger bun

Shaggy Mane
- Edible ☺
- White shaggy cylindrical cap that turns black and inky with age
- Bell shape - mature
- Spore print is black

Death Cap
- Poisonous ☹
- Flattened top
- White cap with brownish scales
- Gills are free and white, turning green as they mature

False Morel
- Poisonous ☹
- Red-brown cap - irregularly lobed, like a brain
- Tube-like hollows
- Yellowish spore print
- Smooth with more wrinkles as it ages

Destroying Angel
- Poisonous ☹
- White stalk and gills
- White cap or white edge and yellowish, pinkish, or tan center
- Egg-shaped cap

Common Conecap
- Poisonous ☹
- Rust-colored brown gills and conical cap
- Surface smooth, dry
- Adnexed gills
- Slender straight stem
- Brown spore print

Deadly Galerina
- Poisonous ☹
- Brownish, sticky cap, yellowish to rusty gills, ring on stalk
- Edges are curved against gills
- Gills narrow, crowded

Lobster Mushroom
- Edible ☺
- Bumpy, reddish-orange exterior
- Fish-like taste
- Irregular shape with little to no stem
- Cracked cap

King Bolete
- Edible ☺
- Light brown to reddish brown
- Stem very thick and club shaped
- White closely spaced small pores
- White flesh

Spore Print

Notes

Location

Site / GPS: _____ Date: _____

◯ Living Tree ◯ Leaf Litter ◯ Mulch ◯ Dead Tree or Wood ◯ Grass
◯ Soil ◯ Other _____

Type of Tree(s) On or Near: _____

Forest Type: ◯ Deciduous ◯ Coniferous ◯ Tropical ◯ Other _____

Weather Conditions: _____

General

Size (overall height): _____ Color: _____ Spore Color: _____

Texture: ◯ Tough ◯ Brittle ◯ Leathery ◯ Woody ◯ Soft ◯ Slimy
◯ Spongy ◯ Powdery ◯ Waxy ◯ Rubbery ◯ Watery (Other) _____

Bruising When Touched? ◯ Yes ◯ No   Notes: _____

Structures: ◯ Cup ◯ Ring ◯ Warts   _____

Cap Characteristics

Campanulate (bell-shaped)

Conical (triangular)

Cylindrical (shaped like half an egg)

Convex (outwardly rounded)

Flat (with top of uniform height)

Infundibuliform (deeply, depressed, funnel-shaped)

Depressed (with a low central region)

Umbonate (with a central bump or knob)

Surface Markings (warts, scales, slime, etc.): _____

Cap Margin: Smooth, Inrolled, Sinuous/Wavy, Other: _____

Color Changes: _____

Undercap

Gills ◯
Attachment: Free or Decurrent
Spacing: Crowded, Close, Distant, Subdistant
Color/Bruising: _____

Pores ◯
Color: _____
Pore Size: _____
Pore Pattern: _____

Teeth ◯
Color: _____
Teeth Length: _____
Flesh: Soft or Tough

Gill Attachment

- ○ Free (gills not attached to stem)
- ○ Adnexed (gills attached narrowly to stem)
- ○ Sinuate (gills smoothly notched and running briefly down stem)
- ○ Adnate (gills widely attached widely to stem)
- ○ Descending (gills running down stem for some length)

Stem Shape

- Tapering
- Equal
- Club-Shaped
- Bulbous
- Cup (volva)

Common Mushrooms

Chanterelle
- Edible ☺
- Shape looks like bell of a trumpet
- Bright yellow/orange
- Similar look to Jack o'Lantern

Milk Mushroom
- Edible ☺
- Rounded caps that connect to an elongated, thick stem
- Smooth firm cap
- Color is pure white

Morels
- Edible ☺
- Honeycombed cap
- Most morels cap is longer than stem
- Spore print is usually light colored
- Interior is hollow

Porcini
- Edible ☺
- Large size
- Also known as king bolete
- Resembles reddish/brown hamburger bun

Shaggy Mane
- Edible ☺
- White shaggy cylindrical cap that turns black and inky with age
- Bell shape - mature
- Spore print is black

Death Cap
- Poisonous ☹
- Flattened top
- White cap with brownish scales
- Gills are free and white, turning green as they mature

False Morel
- Poisonous ☹
- Red-brown cap - irregularly lobed, like a brain
- Tube-like hollows
- Yellowish spore print
- Smooth with more wrinkles as it ages

Destroying Angel
- Poisonous ☹
- White stalk and gills
- White cap or white edge and yellowish, pinkish, or tan center
- Egg-shaped cap

Common Conecap
- Poisonous ☹
- Rust-colored brown gills and conical cap
- Surface smooth, dry
- Adnexed gills
- Slender straight stem
- Brown spore print

Deadly Galerina
- Poisonous ☹
- Brownish, sticky cap, yellowish to rusty gills, ring on stalk
- Edges are curved against gills
- Gills narrow, crowded

Lobster Mushroom
- Edible ☺
- Bumpy, reddish-orange exterior
- Fish-like taste
- Irregular shape with little to no stem
- Cracked cap

King Bolete
- Edible ☺
- Light brown to reddish brown
- Stem very thick and club shaped
- White closely spaced small pores
- White flesh

Spore Print

Notes

Location

Site / GPS: _____ Date: _____

○ Living Tree ○ Leaf Litter ○ Mulch ○ Dead Tree or Wood ○ Grass
○ Soil ○ Other _____

Type of Tree(s) On or Near: _____

Forest Type: ○ Deciduous ○ Coniferous ○ Tropical ○ Other _____

Weather Conditions: _____

General

Size (overall height): _____ Color: _____ Spore Color: _____

Texture: ○ Tough ○ Brittle ○ Leathery ○ Woody ○ Soft ○ Slimy
○ Spongy ○ Powdery ○ Waxy ○ Rubbery ○ Watery (Other) _____

Bruising When Touched? ○ Yes ○ No   Notes: _____

Structures: ○ Cup ○ Ring ○ Warts

Cap Characteristics

Campanulate (bell-shaped)

Conical (triangular)

Cylindrical (shaped like half an egg)

Convex (outwardly rounded)

Flat (with top of uniform height)

Infundibuliform (deeply, depressed, funnel-shaped)

Depressed (with a low central region)

Umbonate (with a central bump or knob)

Surface Markings (warts, scales, slime, etc.): _____

Cap Margin: Smooth, Inrolled, Sinuous/Wavy, Other: _____

Color Changes: _____

Undercap

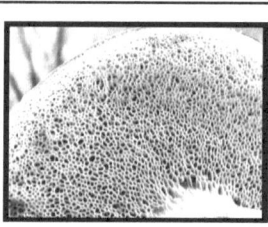

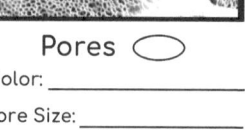

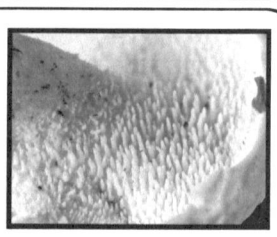

Gills ○
Attachment: Free or Decurrent
Spacing: Crowded, Close, Distant, Subdistant
Color/Bruising: _____

Pores ○
Color: _____
Pore Size: _____
Pore Pattern: _____

Teeth ○
Color: _____
Teeth Length: _____
Flesh: Soft or Tough

Gill Attachment

○ Free
(gills not attached to stem)

○ Adnexed
(gills attached narrowly to stem)

○ Sinuate
(gills smoothly notched and running briefly down stem)

○ Adnate
(gills widely attached widely to stem)

○ Descending
(gills running down stem for some length)

Stem Shape

    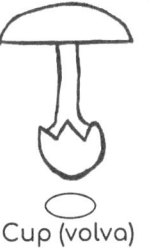

Tapering   Equal   Club-Shaped   Bulbous   Cup (volva)

Common Mushrooms

Chanterelle
- Edible ☺
- Shape looks like bell of a trumpet
- Bright yellow/orange
- Similar look to Jack o'Lantern

Milk Mushroom
- Edible ☺
- Rounded caps that connect to an elongated, thick stem
- Smooth firm cap
- Color is pure white

Morels
- Edible ☺
- Honeycombed cap
- Most morels cap is longer than stem
- Spore print is usually light colored
- Interior is hollow

Porcini
- Edible ☺
- Large size
- Also known as king bolete
- Resembles reddish/brown hamburger bun

Shaggy Mane
- Edible ☺
- White shaggy cylindrical cap that turns black and inky with age
- Bell shape - mature
- Spore print is black

Death Cap
- Poisonous ☹
- Flattened top
- White cap with brownish scales
- Gills are free and white, turning green as they mature

False Morel
- Poisonous ☹
- Red-brown cap - irregularly lobed, like a brain
- Tube-like hollows
- Yellowish spore print
- Smooth with more wrinkles as it ages

Destroying Angel
- Poisonous ☹
- White stalk and gills
- White cap or white edge and yellowish, pinkish, or tan center
- Egg-shaped cap

Common Conecap
- Poisonous ☹
- Rust-colored brown gills and conical cap
- Surface smooth, dry
- Adnexed gills
- Slender straight stem
- Brown spore print

Deadly Galerina
- Poisonous ☹
- Brownish, sticky cap, yellowish to rusty gills, ring on stalk
- Edges are curved against gills
- Gills narrow, crowded

Lobster Mushroom
- Edible ☺
- Bumpy, reddish-orange exterior
- Fish-like taste
- Irregular shape with little to no stem
- Cracked cap

King Bolete
- Edible ☺
- Light brown to reddish brown
- Stem very thick and club shaped
- White closely spaced small pores
- White flesh

Spore Print

_____
_____
_____
_____
_____
_____

Notes

Location

Site / GPS: _____ Date: _____

○ Living Tree ○ Leaf Litter ○ Mulch ○ Dead Tree or Wood ○ Grass
○ Soil ○ Other _____

Type of Tree(s) On or Near: _____

Forest Type: ○ Deciduous ○ Coniferous ○ Tropical ○ Other _____

Weather Conditions: _____

General

Size (overall height): _____ Color: _____ Spore Color: _____

Texture: ○ Tough ○ Brittle ○ Leathery ○ Woody ○ Soft ○ Slimy
○ Spongy ○ Powdery ○ Waxy ○ Rubbery ○ Watery (Other) _____

Bruising When Touched? ○ Yes ○ No Notes: _____

Structures: ○ Cup ○ Ring ○ Warts

Cap Characteristics

Campanulate (bell-shaped)

Conical (triangular)

Cylindrical (shaped like half an egg)

Convex (outwardly rounded)

Flat (with top of uniform height)

Infundibuliform (deeply, depressed, funnel-shaped)

Depressed (with a low central region)

Umbonate (with a central bump or knob)

Surface Markings (warts, scales, slime, etc.): _____

Cap Margin: Smooth, Inrolled, Sinuous/Wavy, Other: _____

Color Changes: _____

Undercap

Gills ○
Attachment: Free or Decurrent
Spacing: Crowded, Close, Distant, Subdistant
Color/Bruising: _____

Pores ○
Color: _____
Pore Size: _____
Pore Pattern: _____

Teeth ○
Color: _____
Teeth Length: _____
Flesh: Soft or Tough

Gill Attachment

○ Free
(gills not attached to stem)

○ Adnexed
(gills attached narrowly to stem)

○ Sinuate
(gills smoothly notched and running briefly down stem)

○ Adnate
(gills widely attached widely to stem)

○ Descending
(gills running down stem for some length)

Stem Shape

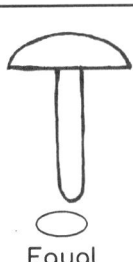   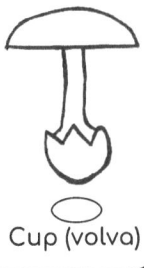

Tapering | Equal | Club-Shaped | Bulbous | Cup (volva)

Common Mushrooms

Chanterelle
- Edible ☺
- Shape looks like bell of a trumpet
- Bright yellow/orange
- Similar look to Jack o'Lantern

Shaggy Mane
- Edible ☺
- White shaggy cylindrical cap that turns black and inky with age
- Bell shape - mature
- Spore print is black

Common Conecap
- Poisonous ☹
- Rust-colored brown gills and conical cap
- Surface smooth, dry
- Adnexed gills
- Slender straight stem
- Brown spore print

Milk Mushroom
- Edible ☺
- Rounded caps that connect to an elongated, thick stem
- Smooth firm cap
- Color is pure white

Death Cap
- Poisonous ☹
- Flattened top
- White cap with brownish scales
- Gills are free and white, turning green as they mature

Deadly Galerina
- Poisonous ☹
- Brownish, sticky cap, yellowish to rusty gills, ring on stalk
- Edges are curved against gills
- Gills narrow, crowded

Morels
- Edible ☺
- Honeycombed cap
- Most morels cap is longer than stem
- Spore print is usually light colored
- Interior is hollow

False Morel
- Poisonous ☹
- Red-brown cap - irregularly lobed, like a brain
- Tube-like hollows
- Yellowish spore print
- Smooth with more wrinkles as it ages

Lobster Mushroom
- Edible ☺
- Bumpy, reddish-orange exterior
- Fish-like taste
- Irregular shape with little to no stem
- Cracked cap

Porcini
- Edible ☺
- Large size
- Also known as king bolete
- Resembles reddish/brown hamburger bun

Destroying Angel
- Poisonous ☹
- White stalk and gills
- White cap or white edge and yellowish, pinkish, or tan center
- Egg-shaped cap

King Bolete
- Edible ☺
- Light brown to reddish brown
- Stem very thick and club shaped
- White closely spaced small pores
- White flesh

Spore Print / Notes

_____
_____
_____
_____
_____
_____

Location

Site / GPS: _____ Date: _____

○ Living Tree ○ Leaf Litter ○ Mulch ○ Dead Tree or Wood ○ Grass
○ Soil ○ Other _____

Type of Tree(s) On or Near: _____

Forest Type: ○ Deciduous ○ Coniferous ○ Tropical ○ Other _____

Weather Conditions: _____

General

Size (overall height): _____ Color: _____ Spore Color: _____

Texture: ○ Tough ○ Brittle ○ Leathery ○ Woody ○ Soft ○ Slimy
○ Spongy ○ Powdery ○ Waxy ○ Rubbery ○ Watery (Other) _____

Bruising When Touched? ○ Yes ○ No   Notes: _____

Structures: ○ Cup ○ Ring ○ Warts

Cap Characteristics

Campanulate (bell-shaped)

Conical (triangular)

Cylindrical (shaped like half an egg)

Convex (outwardly rounded)

Flat (with top of uniform height)

Infundibuliform (deeply, depressed, funnel-shaped)

Depressed (with a low central region)

Umbonate (with a central bump or knob)

Surface Markings (warts, scales, slime, etc.): _____

Cap Margin: Smooth, Inrolled, Sinuous/Wavy, Other: _____

Color Changes: _____

Undercap

Gills ○
Attachment: Free or Decurrent
Spacing: Crowded, Close, Distant, Subdistant
Color/Bruising: _____

Pores ○
Color: _____
Pore Size: _____
Pore Pattern: _____

Teeth ○
Color: _____
Teeth Length: _____
Flesh: Soft or Tough

Gill Attachment

- ○ Free (gills not attached to stem)
- ○ Adnexed (gills attached narrowly to stem)
- ○ Sinuate (gills smoothly notched and running briefly down stem)
- ○ Adnate (gills widely attached widely to stem)
- ○ Descending (gills running down stem for some length)

Stem Shape

- Tapering
- Equal
- Club-Shaped
- Bulbous
- Cup (volva)

Common Mushrooms

Chanterelle
- Edible ☺
- Shape looks like bell of a trumpet
- Bright yellow/orange
- Similar look to Jack o'Lantern

Milk Mushroom
- Edible ☺
- Rounded caps that connect to an elongated, thick stem
- Smooth firm cap
- Color is pure white

Morels
- Edible ☺
- Honeycombed cap
- Most morels cap is longer than stem
- Spore print is usually light colored
- Interior is hollow

Porcini
- Edible ☺
- Large size
- Also known as king bolete
- Resembles reddish/brown hamburger bun

Shaggy Mane
- Edible ☺
- White shaggy cylindrical cap that turns black and inky with age
- Bell shape - mature
- Spore print is black

Death Cap
- Poisonous ☹
- Flattened top
- White cap with brownish scales
- Gills are free and white, turning green as they mature

False Morel
- Poisonous ☹
- Red-brown cap - irregularly lobed, like a brain
- Tube-like hollows
- Yellowish spore print
- Smooth with more wrinkles as it ages

Destroying Angel
- Poisonous ☹
- White stalk and gills
- White cap or white edge and yellowish, pinkish, or tan center
- Egg-shaped cap

Common Conecap
- Poisonous ☹
- Rust-colored brown gills and conical cap
- Surface smooth, dry
- Adnexed gills
- Slender straight stem
- Brown spore print

Deadly Galerina
- Poisonous ☹
- Brownish, sticky cap, yellowish to rusty gills, ring on stalk
- Edges are curved against gills
- Gills narrow, crowded

Lobster Mushroom
- Edible ☺
- Bumpy, reddish-orange exterior
- Fish-like taste
- Irregular shape with little to no stem
- Cracked cap

King Bolete
- Edible ☺
- Light brown to reddish brown
- Stem very thick and club shaped
- White closely spaced small pores
- White flesh

Spore Print

Notes

Location

Site / GPS: _____ Date: _____

○ Living Tree ○ Leaf Litter ○ Mulch ○ Dead Tree or Wood ○ Grass
○ Soil ○ Other _____

Type of Tree(s) On or Near: _____

Forest Type: ○ Deciduous ○ Coniferous ○ Tropical ○ Other _____

Weather Conditions: _____

General

Size (overall height): _____ Color: _____ Spore Color: _____

Texture: ○ Tough ○ Brittle ○ Leathery ○ Woody ○ Soft ○ Slimy
○ Spongy ○ Powdery ○ Waxy ○ Rubbery ○ Watery (Other) _____

Bruising When Touched? ○ Yes ○ No Notes: _____

Structures: ○ Cup ○ Ring ○ Warts

Cap Characteristics

Campanulate (bell-shaped)

Conical (triangular)

Cylindrical (shaped like half an egg)

Convex (outwardly rounded)

Flat (with top of uniform height)

Infundibuliform (deeply, depressed, funnel-shaped)

Depressed (with a low central region)

Umbonate (with a central bump or knob)

Surface Markings (warts, scales, slime, etc.): _____

Cap Margin: Smooth, Inrolled, Sinuous/Wavy, Other: _____

Color Changes: _____

Undercap

Gills ○
Attachment: Free or Decurrent
Spacing: Crowded, Close, Distant, Subdistant
Color/Bruising: _____

Pores ○
Color: _____
Pore Size: _____
Pore Pattern: _____

Teeth ○
Color: _____
Teeth Length: _____
Flesh: Soft or Tough

Gill Attachment

- ○ Free (gills not attached to stem)
- ○ Adnexed (gills attached narrowly to stem)
- ○ Sinuate (gills smoothly notched and running briefly down stem)
- ○ Adnate (gills widely attached widely to stem)
- ○ Descending (gills running down stem for some length)

Stem Shape

    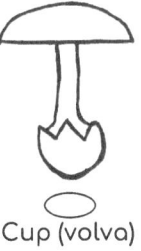

- ○ Tapering
- ○ Equal
- ○ Club-Shaped
- ○ Bulbous
- ○ Cup (volva)

Common Mushrooms

Chanterelle
- Edible ☺
- Shape looks like bell of a trumpet
- Bright yellow/orange
- Similar look to Jack o'Lantern

Milk Mushroom
- Edible ☺
- Rounded caps that connect to an elongated, thick stem
- Smooth firm cap
- Color is pure white

Morels
- Edible ☺
- Honeycombed cap
- Most morels cap is longer than stem
- Spore print is usually light colored
- Interior is hollow

Porcini
- Edible ☺
- Large size
- Also known as king bolete
- Resembles reddish/brown hamburger bun

Shaggy Mane
- Edible ☺
- White shaggy cylindrical cap that turns black and inky with age
- Bell shape - mature
- Spore print is black

Death Cap
- Poisonous ☹
- Flattened top
- White cap with brownish scales
- Gills are free and white, turning green as they mature

False Morel
- Poisonous ☹
- Red-brown cap - irregularly lobed, like a brain
- Tube-like hollows
- Yellowish spore print
- Smooth with more wrinkles as it ages

Destroying Angel
- Poisonous ☹
- White stalk and gills
- White cap or white edge and yellowish, pinkish, or tan center
- Egg-shaped cap

Common Conecap
- Poisonous ☹
- Rust-colored brown gills and conical cap
- Surface smooth, dry
- Adnexed gills
- Slender straight stem
- Brown spore print

Deadly Galerina
- Poisonous ☹
- Brownish, sticky cap, yellowish to rusty gills, ring on stalk
- Edges are curved against gills
- Gills narrow, crowded

Lobster Mushroom
- Edible ☺
- Bumpy, reddish-orange exterior
- Fish-like taste
- Irregular shape with little to no stem
- Cracked cap

King Bolete
- Edible ☺
- Light brown to reddish brown
- Stem very thick and club shaped
- White closely spaced small pores
- White flesh

Spore Print

Notes

Location

Site / GPS: _____ Date: _____

○ Living Tree ○ Leaf Litter ○ Mulch ○ Dead Tree or Wood ○ Grass
○ Soil ○ Other _____

Type of Tree(s) On or Near: _____

Forest Type: ○ Deciduous ○ Coniferous ○ Tropical ○ Other _____

Weather Conditions: _____

General

Size (overall height): _____ Color: _____ Spore Color: _____

Texture: ○ Tough ○ Brittle ○ Leathery ○ Woody ○ Soft ○ Slimy
○ Spongy ○ Powdery ○ Waxy ○ Rubbery ○ Watery (Other) _____

Bruising When Touched? ○ Yes ○ No   Notes: _____

Structures: ○ Cup ○ Ring ○ Warts   _____

Cap Characteristics

Campanulate (bell-shaped)

Conical (triangular)

Cylindrical (shaped like half an egg)

Convex (outwardly rounded)

Flat (with top of uniform height)

Infundibuliform (deeply, depressed, funnel-shaped)

Depressed (with a low central region)

Umbonate (with a central bump or knob)

Surface Markings (warts, scales, slime, etc.): _____

Cap Margin: Smooth, Inrolled, Sinuous/Wavy, Other: _____

Color Changes: _____

Undercap

Gills ○
Attachment: Free or Decurrent
Spacing: Crowded, Close, Distant, Subdistant
Color/Bruising: _____

Pores ○
Color: _____
Pore Size: _____
Pore Pattern: _____

Teeth ○
Color: _____
Teeth Length: _____
Flesh: Soft or Tough

Gill Attachment

- Free (gills not attached to stem)
- Adnexed (gills attached narrowly to stem)
- Sinuate (gills smoothly notched and running briefly down stem)
- Adnate (gills widely attached widely to stem)
- Descending (gills running down stem for some length)

Stem Shape

- Tapering
- Equal
- Club-Shaped
- Bulbous
- Cup (volva)

Common Mushrooms

Chanterelle
- Edible ☺
- Shape looks like bell of a trumpet
- Bright yellow/orange
- Similar look to Jack o'Lantern

Shaggy Mane
- Edible ☺
- White shaggy cylindrical cap that turns black and inky with age
- Bell shape - mature
- Spore print is black

Common Conecap
- Poisonous ☹
- Rust-colored brown gills and conical cap
- Surface smooth, dry
- Adnexed gills
- Slender straight stem
- Brown spore print

Milk Mushroom
- Edible ☺
- Rounded caps that connect to an elongated, thick stem
- Smooth firm cap
- Color is pure white

Death Cap
- Poisonous ☹
- Flattened top
- White cap with brownish scales
- Gills are free and white, turning green as they mature

Deadly Galerina
- Poisonous ☹
- Brownish, sticky cap, yellowish to rusty gills, ring on stalk
- Edges are curved against gills
- Gills narrow, crowded

Morels
- Edible ☺
- Honeycombed cap
- Most morels cap is longer than stem
- Spore print is usually light colored
- Interior is hollow

False Morel
- Poisonous ☹
- Red-brown cap - irregularly lobed, like a brain
- Tube-like hollows
- Yellowish spore print
- Smooth with more wrinkles as it ages

Lobster Mushroom
- Edible ☺
- Bumpy, reddish-orange exterior
- Fish-like taste
- Irregular shape with little to no stem
- Cracked cap

Porcini
- Edible ☺
- Large size
- Also known as king bolete
- Resembles reddish/brown hamburger bun

Destroying Angel
- Poisonous ☹
- White stalk and gills
- White cap or white edge and yellowish, pinkish, or tan center
- Egg-shaped cap

King Bolete
- Edible ☺
- Light brown to reddish brown
- Stem very thick and club shaped
- White closely spaced small pores
- White flesh

Spore Print

Notes

_____
_____
_____
_____
_____

Location

Site / GPS: _____ Date: _____

○ Living Tree ○ Leaf Litter ○ Mulch ○ Dead Tree or Wood ○ Grass
○ Soil ○ Other _____

Type of Tree(s) On or Near: _____

Forest Type: ○ Deciduous ○ Coniferous ○ Tropical ○ Other _____

Weather Conditions: _____

General

Size (overall height): _____ Color: _____ Spore Color: _____

Texture: ○ Tough ○ Brittle ○ Leathery ○ Woody ○ Soft ○ Slimy
○ Spongy ○ Powdery ○ Waxy ○ Rubbery ○ Watery (Other) _____

Bruising When Touched? ○ Yes ○ No Notes: _____

Structures: ○ Cup ○ Ring ○ Warts

Cap Characteristics

Campanulate (bell-shaped)

Conical (triangular)

Cylindrical (shaped like half an egg)

Convex (outwardly rounded)

Flat (with top of uniform height)

Infundibuliform (deeply, depressed, funnel-shaped)

Depressed (with a low central region)

Umbonate (with a central bump or knob)

Surface Markings (warts, scales, slime, etc.): _____

Cap Margin: Smooth, Inrolled, Sinuous/Wavy, Other: _____

Color Changes: _____

Undercap

Gills ○
Attachment: Free or Decurrent
Spacing: Crowded, Close, Distant, Subdistant
Color/Bruising: _____

Pores ○
Color: _____
Pore Size: _____
Pore Pattern: _____

Teeth ○
Color: _____
Teeth Length: _____
Flesh: Soft or Tough

Gill Attachment

- ○ Free (gills not attached to stem)
- ○ Adnexed (gills attached narrowly to stem)
- ○ Sinuate (gills smoothly notched and running briefly down stem)
- ○ Adnate (gills widely attached widely to stem)
- ○ Descending (gills running down stem for some length)

Stem Shape

   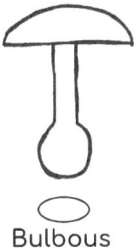 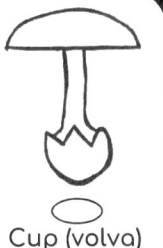

Tapering — Equal — Club-Shaped — Bulbous — Cup (volva)

Common Mushrooms

Chanterelle
- Edible ☺
- Shape looks like bell of a trumpet
- Bright yellow/orange
- Similar look to Jack o'Lantern

Shaggy Mane
- Edible ☺
- White shaggy cylindrical cap that turns black and inky with age
- Bell shape - mature
- Spore print is black

Common Conecap
- Poisonous ☹
- Rust-colored brown gills and conical cap
- Surface smooth, dry
- Adnexed gills
- Slender straight stem
- Brown spore print

Milk Mushroom
- Edible ☺
- Rounded caps that connect to an elongated, thick stem
- Smooth firm cap
- Color is pure white

Death Cap
- Poisonous ☹
- Flattened top
- White cap with brownish scales
- Gills are free and white, turning green as they mature

Deadly Galerina
- Poisonous ☹
- Brownish, sticky cap, yellowish to rusty gills, ring on stalk
- Edges are curved against gills
- Gills narrow, crowded

Morels
- Edible ☺
- Honeycombed cap
- Most morels cap is longer than stem
- Spore print is usually light colored
- Interior is hollow

False Morel
- Poisonous ☹
- Red-brown cap - irregularly lobed, like a brain
- Tube-like hollows
- Yellowish spore print
- Smooth with more wrinkles as it ages

Lobster Mushroom
- Edible ☺
- Bumpy, reddish-orange exterior
- Fish-like taste
- Irregular shape with little to no stem
- Cracked cap

Porcini
- Edible ☺
- Large size
- Also known as king bolete
- Resembles reddish/brown hamburger bun

Destroying Angel
- Poisonous ☹
- White stalk and gills
- White cap or white edge and yellowish, pinkish, or tan center
- Egg-shaped cap

King Bolete
- Edible ☺
- Light brown to reddish brown
- Stem very thick and club shaped
- White closely spaced small pores
- White flesh

Spore Print

Notes

_____
_____
_____
_____
_____
_____

Location

Site / GPS: _____ Date: _____

○ Living Tree ○ Leaf Litter ○ Mulch ○ Dead Tree or Wood ○ Grass
○ Soil ○ Other _____

Type of Tree(s) On or Near: _____

Forest Type: ○ Deciduous ○ Coniferous ○ Tropical ○ Other _____

Weather Conditions: _____

General

Size (overall height): _____ Color: _____ Spore Color: _____

Texture: ○ Tough ○ Brittle ○ Leathery ○ Woody ○ Soft ○ Slimy
○ Spongy ○ Powdery ○ Waxy ○ Rubbery ○ Watery (Other) _____

Bruising When Touched? ○ Yes ○ No   Notes: _____

Structures: ○ Cup ○ Ring ○ Warts

Cap Characteristics

Campanulate (bell-shaped)

Conical (triangular)

Cylindrical (shaped like half an egg)

Convex (outwardly rounded)

Flat (with top of uniform height)

Infundibuliform (deeply, depressed, funnel-shaped)

Depressed (with a low central region)

Umbonate (with a central bump or knob)

Surface Markings (warts, scales, slime, etc.): _____

Cap Margin: Smooth, Inrolled, Sinuous/Wavy, Other: _____

Color Changes: _____

Undercap

Gills ○
Attachment: Free or Decurrent
Spacing: Crowded, Close, Distant, Subdistant
Color/Bruising: _____

Pores ○
Color: _____
Pore Size: _____
Pore Pattern: _____

Teeth ○
Color: _____
Teeth Length: _____
Flesh: Soft or Tough

Gill Attachment

○ Free
(gills not attached to stem)

○ Adnexed
(gills attached narrowly to stem)

○ Sinuate
(gills smoothly notched and running briefly down stem)

○ Adnate
(gills widely attached widely to stem)

○ Descenting
(gills running down stem for some length)

Stem Shape

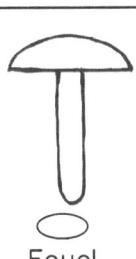   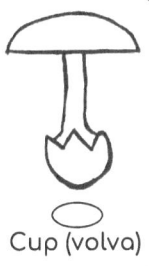

○ Tapering   ○ Equal   ○ Club-Shaped   ○ Bulbous   ○ Cup (volva)

Common Mushrooms

Chanterelle
- Edible 😊
- Shape looks like bell of a trumpet
- Bright yellow/orange
- Similar look to Jack o'Lantern

Shaggy Mane
- Edible 😊
- White shaggy cylindrical cap that turns black and inky with age
- Bell shape - mature
- Spore print is black

Common Conecap
- Poisonous 😖
- Rust-colored brown gills and conical cap
- Surface smooth, dry
- Adnexed gills
- Slender straight stem
- Brown spore print

Milk Mushroom
- Edible 😊
- Rounded caps that connect to an elongated, thick stem
- Smooth firm cap
- Color is pure white

Death Cap
- Poisonous 😖
- Flattened top
- White cap with brownish scales
- Gills are free and white, turning green as they mature

Deadly Galerina
- Poisonous 😖
- Brownish, sticky cap, yellowish to rusty gills, ring on stalk
- Edges are curved against gills
- Gills narrow, crowded

Morels
- Edible 😊
- Honeycombed cap
- Most morels cap is longer than stem
- Spore print is usually light colored
- Interior is hollow

False Morel
- Poisonous 😖
- Red-brown cap - irregularly lobed, like a brain
- Tube-like hollows
- Yellowish spore print
- Smooth with more wrinkles as it ages

Lobster Mushroom
- Edible 😊
- Bumpy, reddish-orange exterior
- Fish-like taste
- Irregular shape with little to no stem
- Cracked cap

Porcini
- Edible 😊
- Large size
- Also known as king bolete
- Resembles reddish/brown hamburger bun

Destroying Angel
- Poisonous 😖
- White stalk and gills
- White cap or white edge and yellowish, pinkish, or tan center
- Egg-shaped cap

King Bolete
- Edible 😊
- Light brown to reddish brown
- Stem very thick and club shaped
- White closely spaced small pores
- White flesh

Spore Print

Notes

_____
_____
_____
_____
_____
_____

Location

Site / GPS: _____ Date: _____

◯ Living Tree ◯ Leaf Litter ◯ Mulch ◯ Dead Tree or Wood ◯ Grass
◯ Soil ◯ Other _____

Type of Tree(s) On or Near: _____

Forest Type: ◯ Deciduous ◯ Coniferous ◯ Tropical ◯ Other _____

Weather Conditions: _____

General

Size (overall height): _____ Color: _____ Spore Color: _____

Texture: ◯ Tough ◯ Brittle ◯ Leathery ◯ Woody ◯ Soft ◯ Slimy
◯ Spongy ◯ Powdery ◯ Waxy ◯ Rubbery ◯ Watery (Other) _____

Bruising When Touched? ◯ Yes ◯ No Notes: _____

Structures: ◯ Cup ◯ Ring ◯ Warts _____

Cap Characteristics

Campanulate (bell-shaped)

Conical (triangular)

Cylindrical (shaped like half an egg)

Convex (outwardly rounded)

Flat (with top of uniform height)

Infundibuliform (deeply, depressed, funnel-shaped)

Depressed (with a low central region)

Umbonate (with a central bump or knob)

Surface Markings (warts, scales, slime, etc.): _____

Cap Margin: Smooth, Inrolled, Sinuous/Wavy, Other: _____

Color Changes: _____

Undercap

Gills ◯
Attachment: Free or Decurrent
Spacing: Crowded, Close, Distant, Subdistant
Color/Bruising: _____

Pores ◯
Color: _____
Pore Size: _____
Pore Pattern: _____

Teeth ◯
Color: _____
Teeth Length: _____
Flesh: Soft or Tough

Gill Attachment

- ○ **Free** (gills not attached to stem)
- ○ **Adnexed** (gills attached narrowly to stem)
- ○ **Sinuate** (gills smoothly notched and running briefly down stem)
- ○ **Adnate** (gills widely attached widely to stem)
- ○ **Descending** (gills running down stem for some length)

Stem Shape

    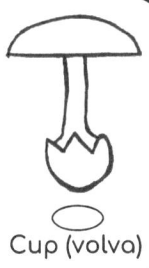

Tapering | Equal | Club-Shaped | Bulbous | Cup (volva)

Common Mushrooms

Chanterelle
- Edible ☺
- Shape looks like bell of a trumpet
- Bright yellow/orange
- Similar look to Jack o'Lantern

Shaggy Mane
- Edible ☺
- White shaggy cylindrical cap that turns black and inky with age
- Bell shape - mature
- Spore print is black

Common Conecap
- Poisonous ☹
- Rust-colored brown gills and conical cap
- Surface smooth, dry
- Adnexed gills
- Slender straight stem
- Brown spore print

Milk Mushroom
- Edible ☺
- Rounded caps that connect to an elongated, thick stem
- Smooth firm cap
- Color is pure white

Death Cap
- Poisonous ☹
- Flattened top
- White cap with brownish scales
- Gills are free and white, turning green as they mature

Deadly Galerina
- Poisonous ☹
- Brownish, sticky cap, yellowish to rusty gills, ring on stalk
- Edges are curved against gills
- Gills narrow, crowded

Morels
- Edible ☺
- Honeycombed cap
- Most morels cap is longer than stem
- Spore print is usually light colored
- Interior is hollow

False Morel
- Poisonous ☹
- Red-brown cap - irregularly lobed, like a brain
- Tube-like hollows
- Yellowish spore print
- Smooth with more wrinkles as it ages

Lobster Mushroom
- Edible ☺
- Bumpy, reddish-orange exterior
- Fish-like taste
- Irregular shape with little to no stem
- Cracked cap

Porcini
- Edible ☺
- Large size
- Also known as king bolete
- Resembles reddish/brown hamburger bun

Destroying Angel
- Poisonous ☹
- White stalk and gills
- White cap or white edge and yellowish, pinkish, or tan center
- Egg-shaped cap

King Bolete
- Edible ☺
- Light brown to reddish brown
- Stem very thick and club shaped
- White closely spaced small pores
- White flesh

Spore Print

_____
_____
_____
_____
_____
_____

Notes

Location

Site / GPS: _____ Date: _____

○ Living Tree ○ Leaf Litter ○ Mulch ○ Dead Tree or Wood ○ Grass
○ Soil ○ Other _____

Type of Tree(s) On or Near: _____

Forest Type: ○ Deciduous ○ Coniferous ○ Tropical ○ Other _____

Weather Conditions: _____

General

Size (overall height): _____ Color: _____ Spore Color: _____

Texture: ○ Tough ○ Brittle ○ Leathery ○ Woody ○ Soft ○ Slimy
○ Spongy ○ Powdery ○ Waxy ○ Rubbery ○ Watery (Other) _____

Bruising When Touched? ○ Yes ○ No Notes: _____

Structures: ○ Cup ○ Ring ○ Warts _____

Cap Characteristics

Campanulate (bell-shaped)

Conical (triangular)

Cylindrical (shaped like half an egg)

Convex (outwardly rounded)

Flat (with top of uniform height)

Infundibuliform (deeply, depressed, funnel-shaped)

Depressed (with a low central region)

Umbonate (with a central bump or knob)

Surface Markings (warts, scales, slime, etc.): _____

Cap Margin: Smooth, Inrolled, Sinuous/Wavy, Other: _____

Color Changes: _____

Undercap

Gills ○
Attachment: Free or Decurrent
Spacing: Crowded, Close, Distant, Subdistant
Color/Bruising: _____

Pores ○
Color: _____
Pore Size: _____
Pore Pattern: _____

Teeth ○
Color: _____
Teeth Length: _____
Flesh: Soft or Tough

Gill Attachment

○ Free
(gills not attached to stem)

○ Adnexed
(gills attached narrowly to stem)

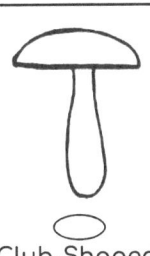

○ Sinuate
(gills smoothly notched and running briefly down stem)

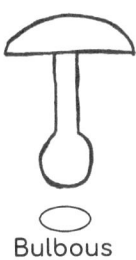

○ Adnate
(gills widely attached widely to stem)

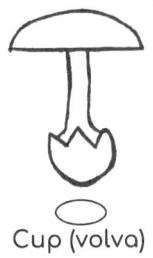

○ Descenting
(gills running down stem for some length)

Stem Shape

Tapering | Equal | Club-Shaped | Bulbous | Cup (volva)

Common Mushrooms

Chanterelle
- Edible ☺
- Shape looks like bell of a trumpet
- Bright yellow/orange
- Similar look to Jack o'Lantern

Shaggy Mane
- Edible ☺
- White shaggy cylindrical cap that turns black and inky with age
- Bell shape - mature
- Spore print is black

Common Conecap
- Poisonous ☹
- Rust-colored brown gills and conical cap
- Surface smooth, dry
- Adnexed gills
- Slender straight stem
- Brown spore print

Milk Mushroom
- Edible ☺
- Rounded caps that connect to an elongated, thick stem
- Smooth firm cap
- Color is pure white

Death Cap
- Poisonous ☹
- Flattened top
- White cap with brownish scales
- Gills are free and white, turning green as they mature

Deadly Galerina
- Poisonous ☹
- Brownish, sticky cap, yellowish to rusty gills, ring on stalk
- Edges are curved against gills
- Gills narrow, crowded

Morels
- Edible ☺
- Honeycombed cap
- Most morels cap is longer than stem
- Spore print is usually light colored
- Interior is hollow

False Morel
- Poisonous ☹
- Red-brown cap - irregularly lobed, like a brain
- Tube-like hollows
- Yellowish spore print
- Smooth with more wrinkles as it ages

Lobster Mushroom
- Edible ☺
- Bumpy, reddish-orange exterior
- Fish-like taste
- Irregular shape with little to no stem
- Cracked cap

Porcini
- Edible ☺
- Large size
- Also known as king bolete
- Resembles reddish/brown hamburger bun

Destroying Angel
- Poisonous ☹
- White stalk and gills
- White cap or white edge and yellowish, pinkish, or tan center
- Egg-shaped cap

King Bolete
- Edible ☺
- Light brown to reddish brown
- Stem very thick and club shaped
- White closely spaced small pores
- White flesh

Spore Print

Notes

Location

Site / GPS: _____ Date: _____

◯ Living Tree ◯ Leaf Litter ◯ Mulch ◯ Dead Tree or Wood ◯ Grass
◯ Soil ◯ Other _____

Type of Tree(s) On or Near: _____

Forest Type: ◯ Deciduous ◯ Coniferous ◯ Tropical ◯ Other _____

Weather Conditions: _____

General

Size (overall height): _____ Color: _____ Spore Color: _____

Texture: ◯ Tough ◯ Brittle ◯ Leathery ◯ Woody ◯ Soft ◯ Slimy
◯ Spongy ◯ Powdery ◯ Waxy ◯ Rubbery ◯ Watery (Other) _____

Bruising When Touched? ◯ Yes ◯ No   Notes: _____

Structures: ◯ Cup ◯ Ring ◯ Warts

Cap Characteristics

Campanulate (bell-shaped)

Conical (triangular)

Cylindrical (shaped like half an egg)

Convex (outwardly rounded)

Flat (with top of uniform height)

Infundibuliform (deeply, depressed, funnel-shaped)

Depressed (with a low central region)

Umbonate (with a central bump or knob)

Surface Markings (warts, scales, slime, etc.): _____

Cap Margin: Smooth, Inrolled, Sinuous/Wavy, Other: _____

Color Changes: _____

Undercap

Gills ◯
Attachment: Free or Decurrent
Spacing: Crowded, Close, Distant, Subdistant
Color/Bruising: _____

Pores ◯
Color: _____
Pore Size: _____
Pore Pattern: _____

Teeth ◯
Color: _____
Teeth Length: _____
Flesh: Soft or Tough

Gill Attachment

- **Free** (gills not attached to stem)
- **Adnexed** (gills attached narrowly to stem)
- **Sinuate** (gills smoothly notched and running briefly down stem)
- **Adnate** (gills widely attached widely to stem)
- **Descending** (gills running down stem for some length)

Stem Shape

    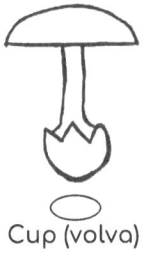

Tapering — Equal — Club-Shaped — Bulbous — Cup (volva)

Common Mushrooms

Chanterelle
- Edible ☺
- Shape looks like bell of a trumpet
- Bright yellow/orange
- Similar look to Jack o'Lantern

Milk Mushroom
- Edible ☺
- Rounded caps that connect to an elongated, thick stem
- Smooth firm cap
- Color is pure white

Morels
- Edible ☺
- Honeycombed cap
- Most morels cap is longer than stem
- Spore print is usually light colored
- Interior is hollow

Porcini
- Edible ☺
- Large size
- Also known as king bolete
- Resembles reddish/brown hamburger bun

Shaggy Mane
- Edible ☺
- White shaggy cylindrical cap that turns black and inky with age
- Bell shape - mature
- Spore print is black

Death Cap
- Poisonous ☹
- Flattened top
- White cap with brownish scales
- Gills are free and white, turning green as they mature

False Morel
- Poisonous ☹
- Red-brown cap - irregularly lobed, like a brain
- Tube-like hollows
- Yellowish spore print
- Smooth with more wrinkles as it ages

Destroying Angel
- Poisonous ☹
- White stalk and gills
- White cap or white edge and yellowish, pinkish, or tan center
- Egg-shaped cap

Common Conecap
- Poisonous ☹
- Rust-colored brown gills and conical cap
- Surface smooth, dry
- Adnexed gills
- Slender straight stem
- Brown spore print

Deadly Galerina
- Poisonous ☹
- Brownish, sticky cap, yellowish to rusty gills, ring on stalk
- Edges are curved against gills
- Gills narrow, crowded

Lobster Mushroom
- Edible ☺
- Bumpy, reddish-orange exterior
- Fish-like taste
- Irregular shape with little to no stem
- Cracked cap

King Bolete
- Edible ☺
- Light brown to reddish brown
- Stem very thick and club shaped
- White closely spaced small pores
- White flesh

Spore Print

Notes

Location

Site / GPS: _____ Date: _____

○ Living Tree ○ Leaf Litter ○ Mulch ○ Dead Tree or Wood ○ Grass
○ Soil ○ Other _____

Type of Tree(s) On or Near: _____

Forest Type: ○ Deciduous ○ Coniferous ○ Tropical ○ Other _____

Weather Conditions: _____

General

Size (overall height): _____ Color: _____ Spore Color: _____

Texture: ○ Tough ○ Brittle ○ Leathery ○ Woody ○ Soft ○ Slimy
○ Spongy ○ Powdery ○ Waxy ○ Rubbery ○ Watery (Other) _____

Bruising When Touched? ○ Yes ○ No   Notes: _____

Structures: ○ Cup ○ Ring ○ Warts

Cap Characteristics

Campanulate (bell-shaped)

Conical (triangular)

Cylindrical (shaped like half an egg)

Convex (outwardly rounded)

Flat (with top of uniform height)

Infundibuliform (deeply, depressed, funnel-shaped)

Depressed (with a low central region)

Umbonate (with a central bump or knob)

Surface Markings (warts, scales, slime, etc.): _____

Cap Margin: Smooth, Inrolled, Sinuous/Wavy, Other: _____

Color Changes: _____

Undercap

Gills ○
Attachment: Free or Decurrent
Spacing: Crowded, Close, Distant, Subdistant
Color/Bruising: _____

Pores ○
Color: _____
Pore Size: _____
Pore Pattern: _____

Teeth ○
Color: _____
Teeth Length: _____
Flesh: Soft or Tough

Gill Attachment

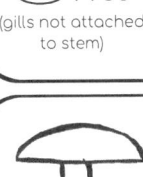

- ◯ Free (gills not attached to stem)
- ◯ Adnexed (gills attached narrowly to stem)
- ◯ Sinuate (gills smoothly notched and running briefly down stem)
- ◯ Adnate (gills widely attached widely to stem)
- ◯ Descending (gills running down stem for some length)

Stem Shape

- Tapering
- Equal
- Club-Shaped
- Bulbous
- Cup (volva)

Common Mushrooms

Chanterelle
- Edible ☺
- Shape looks like bell of a trumpet
- Bright yellow/orange
- Similar look to Jack o'Lantern

Milk Mushroom
- Edible ☺
- Rounded caps that connect to an elongated, thick stem
- Smooth firm cap
- Color is pure white

Morels
- Edible ☺
- Honeycombed cap
- Most morels cap is longer than stem
- Spore print is usually light colored
- Interior is hollow

Porcini
- Edible ☺
- Large size
- Also known as king bolete
- Resembles reddish/brown hamburger bun

Shaggy Mane
- Edible ☺
- White shaggy cylindrical cap that turns black and inky with age
- Bell shape - mature
- Spore print is black

Death Cap
- Poisonous ☹
- Flattened top
- White cap with brownish scales
- Gills are free and white, turning green as they mature

False Morel
- Poisonous ☹
- Red-brown cap - irregularly lobed, like a brain
- Tube-like hollows
- Yellowish spore print
- Smooth with more wrinkles as it ages

Destroying Angel
- Poisonous ☹
- White stalk and gills
- White cap or white edge and yellowish, pinkish, or tan center
- Egg-shaped cap

Common Conecap
- Poisonous ☹
- Rust-colored brown gills and conical cap
- Surface smooth, dry
- Adnexed gills
- Slender straight stem
- Brown spore print

Deadly Galerina
- Poisonous ☹
- Brownish, sticky cap, yellowish to rusty gills, ring on stalk
- Edges are curved against gills
- Gills narrow, crowded

Lobster Mushroom
- Edible ☺
- Bumpy, reddish-orange exterior
- Fish-like taste
- Irregular shape with little to no stem
- Cracked cap

King Bolete
- Edible ☺
- Light brown to reddish brown
- Stem very thick and club shaped
- White closely spaced small pores
- White flesh

Spore Print

Notes

_____
_____
_____
_____
_____
_____

Location

Site / GPS: _____ Date: _____

○ Living Tree ○ Leaf Litter ○ Mulch ○ Dead Tree or Wood ○ Grass
○ Soil ○ Other _____

Type of Tree(s) On or Near: _____

Forest Type: ○ Deciduous ○ Coniferous ○ Tropical ○ Other _____

Weather Conditions: _____

General

Size (overall height): _____ Color: _____ Spore Color: _____

Texture: ○ Tough ○ Brittle ○ Leathery ○ Woody ○ Soft ○ Slimy
○ Spongy ○ Powdery ○ Waxy ○ Rubbery ○ Watery (Other) _____

Bruising When Touched? ○ Yes ○ No Notes: _____

Structures: ○ Cup ○ Ring ○ Warts

Cap Characteristics

Campanulate (bell-shaped)

Conical (triangular)

Cylindrical (shaped like half an egg)

Convex (outwardly rounded)

Flat (with top of uniform height)

Infundibuliform (deeply, depressed, funnel-shaped)

Depressed (with a low central region)

Umbonate (with a central bump or knob)

Surface Markings (warts, scales, slime, etc.): _____

Cap Margin: Smooth, Inrolled, Sinuous/Wavy, Other: _____

Color Changes: _____

Undercap

Gills ○
Attachment: Free or Decurrent
Spacing: Crowded, Close, Distant, Subdistant
Color/Bruising: _____

Pores ○
Color: _____
Pore Size: _____
Pore Pattern: _____

Teeth ○
Color: _____
Teeth Length: _____
Flesh: Soft or Tough

Gill Attachment

- **Free** (gills not attached to stem)
- **Adnexed** (gills attached narrowly to stem)
- **Sinuate** (gills smoothly notched and running briefly down stem)
- **Adnate** (gills widely attached widely to stem)
- **Descending** (gills running down stem for some length)

Stem Shape

    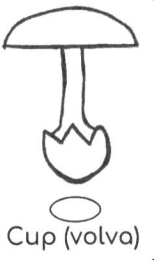

- **Tapering**
- **Equal**
- **Club-Shaped**
- **Bulbous**
- **Cup (volva)**

Common Mushrooms

Chanterelle
- Edible ☺
- Shape looks like bell of a trumpet
- Bright yellow/orange
- Similar look to Jack o'Lantern

Milk Mushroom
- Edible ☺
- Rounded caps that connect to an elongated, thick stem
- Smooth firm cap
- Color is pure white

Morels
- Edible ☺
- Honeycombed cap
- Most morels cap is longer than stem
- Spore print is usually light colored
- Interior is hollow

Porcini
- Edible ☺
- Large size
- Also known as king bolete
- Resembles reddish/brown hamburger bun

Shaggy Mane
- Edible ☺
- White shaggy cylindrical cap that turns black and inky with age
- Bell shape - mature
- Spore print is black

Death Cap
- Poisonous ☹
- Flattened top
- White cap with brownish scales
- Gills are free and white, turning green as they mature

False Morel
- Poisonous ☹
- Red-brown cap - irregularly lobed, like a brain
- Tube-like hollows
- Yellowish spore print
- Smooth with more wrinkles as it ages

Destroying Angel
- Poisonous ☹
- White stalk and gills
- White cap or white edge and yellowish, pinkish, or tan center
- Egg-shaped cap

Common Conecap
- Poisonous ☹
- Rust-colored brown gills and conical cap
- Surface smooth, dry
- Adnexed gills
- Slender straight stem
- Brown spore print

Deadly Galerina
- Poisonous ☹
- Brownish, sticky cap, yellowish to rusty gills, ring on stalk
- Edges are curved against gills
- Gills narrow, crowded

Lobster Mushroom
- Edible ☺
- Bumpy, reddish-orange exterior
- Fish-like taste
- Irregular shape with little to no stem
- Cracked cap

King Bolete
- Edible ☺
- Light brown to reddish brown
- Stem very thick and club shaped
- White closely spaced small pores
- White flesh

Spore Print

Notes

Location

Site / GPS: _____ Date: _____

○ Living Tree ○ Leaf Litter ○ Mulch ○ Dead Tree or Wood ○ Grass
○ Soil ○ Other _____

Type of Tree(s) On or Near: _____

Forest Type: ○ Deciduous ○ Coniferous ○ Tropical ○ Other _____

Weather Conditions: _____

General

Size (overall height): _____ Color: _____ Spore Color: _____

Texture: ○ Tough ○ Brittle ○ Leathery ○ Woody ○ Soft ○ Slimy
○ Spongy ○ Powdery ○ Waxy ○ Rubbery ○ Watery (Other) _____

Bruising When Touched? ○ Yes ○ No   Notes: _____

Structures: ○ Cup ○ Ring ○ Warts   _____

Cap Characteristics

Campanulate (bell-shaped)

Conical (triangular)

Cylindrical (shaped like half an egg)

Convex (outwardly rounded)

Flat (with top of uniform height)

Infundibuliform (deeply, depressed, funnel-shaped)

Depressed (with a low central region)

Umbonate (with a central bump or knob)

Surface Markings (warts, scales, slime, etc.): _____

Cap Margin: Smooth, Inrolled, Sinuous/Wavy, Other: _____

Color Changes: _____

Undercap

Gills ○
Attachment: Free or Decurrent
Spacing: Crowded, Close, Distant, Subdistant
Color/Bruising: _____

Pores ○
Color: _____
Pore Size: _____
Pore Pattern: _____

Teeth ○
Color: _____
Teeth Length: _____
Flesh: Soft or Tough

Gill Attachment

- ○ Free (gills not attached to stem)
- ○ Adnexed (gills attached narrowly to stem)
- ○ Sinuate (gills smoothly notched and running briefly down stem)
- ○ Adnate (gills widely attached widely to stem)
- ○ Descending (gills running down stem for some length)

Stem Shape

- Tapering
- Equal
- Club-Shaped
- Bulbous
- Cup (volva)

Common Mushrooms

Chanterelle
- Edible ☺
- Shape looks like bell of a trumpet
- Bright yellow/orange
- Similar look to Jack o'Lantern

Milk Mushroom
- Edible ☺
- Rounded caps that connect to an elongated, thick stem
- Smooth firm cap
- Color is pure white

Morels
- Edible ☺
- Honeycombed cap
- Most morels cap is longer than stem
- Spore print is usually light colored
- Interior is hollow

Porcini
- Edible ☺
- Large size
- Also known as king bolete
- Resembles reddish/brown hamburger bun

Shaggy Mane
- Edible ☺
- White shaggy cylindrical cap that turns black and inky with age
- Bell shape - mature
- Spore print is black

Death Cap
- Poisonous ☹
- Flattened top
- White cap with brownish scales
- Gills are free and white, turning green as they mature

False Morel
- Poisonous ☹
- Red-brown cap - irregularly lobed, like a brain
- Tube-like hollows
- Yellowish spore print
- Smooth with more wrinkles as it ages

Destroying Angel
- Poisonous ☹
- White stalk and gills
- White cap or white edge and yellowish, pinkish, or tan center
- Egg-shaped cap

Common Conecap
- Poisonous ☹
- Rust-colored brown gills and conical cap
- Surface smooth, dry
- Adnexed gills
- Slender straight stem
- Brown spore print

Deadly Galerina
- Poisonous ☹
- Brownish, sticky cap, yellowish to rusty gills, ring on stalk
- Edges are curved against gills
- Gills narrow, crowded

Lobster Mushroom
- Edible ☺
- Bumpy, reddish-orange exterior
- Fish-like taste
- Irregular shape with little to no stem
- Cracked cap

King Bolete
- Edible ☺
- Light brown to reddish brown
- Stem very thick and club shaped
- White closely spaced small pores
- White flesh

Spore Print

Notes

Location

Site / GPS: _____ Date: _____

○ Living Tree ○ Leaf Litter ○ Mulch ○ Dead Tree or Wood ○ Grass
○ Soil ○ Other _____

Type of Tree(s) On or Near: _____

Forest Type: ○ Deciduous ○ Coniferous ○ Tropical ○ Other _____

Weather Conditions: _____

General

Size (overall height): _____ Color: _____ Spore Color: _____

Texture: ○ Tough ○ Brittle ○ Leathery ○ Woody ○ Soft ○ Slimy
○ Spongy ○ Powdery ○ Waxy ○ Rubbery ○ Watery (Other) _____

Bruising When Touched? ○ Yes ○ No   Notes: _____

Structures: ○ Cup ○ Ring ○ Warts

Cap Characteristics

Campanulate (bell-shaped)

Conical (triangular)

Cylindrical (shaped like half an egg)

Convex (outwardly rounded)

Flat (with top of uniform height)

Infundibuliform (deeply, depressed, funnel-shaped)

Depressed (with a low central region)

Umbonate (with a central bump or knob)

Surface Markings (warts, scales, slime, etc.): _____

Cap Margin: Smooth, Inrolled, Sinuous/Wavy, Other: _____

Color Changes: _____

Undercap

Gills ○
Attachment: Free or Decurrent
Spacing: Crowded, Close, Distant, Subdistant
Color/Bruising: _____

Pores ○
Color: _____
Pore Size: _____
Pore Pattern: _____

Teeth ○
Color: _____
Teeth Length: _____
Flesh: Soft or Tough

Gill Attachment

 ○ **Free**
(gills not attached to stem)

 ○ **Adnexed**
(gills attached narrowly to stem)

 ○ **Sinuate**
(gills smoothly notched and running briefly down stem)

 ○ **Adnate**
(gills widely attached widely to stem)

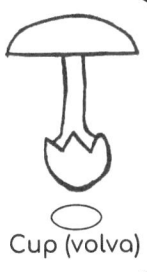 ○ **Descending**
(gills running down stem for some length)

Stem Shape

Tapering — Equal — Club-Shaped — Bulbous — Cup (volva)

Common Mushrooms

Chanterelle
- Edible ☺
- Shape looks like bell of a trumpet
- Bright yellow/orange
- Similar look to Jack o'Lantern

Milk Mushroom
- Edible ☺
- Rounded caps that connect to an elongated, thick stem
- Smooth firm cap
- Color is pure white

Morels
- Edible ☺
- Honeycombed cap
- Most morels cap is longer than stem
- Spore print is usually light colored
- Interior is hollow

Porcini
- Edible ☺
- Large size
- Also known as king bolete
- Resembles reddish/brown hamburger bun

Shaggy Mane
- Edible ☺
- White shaggy cylindrical cap that turns black and inky with age
- Bell shape - mature
- Spore print is black

Death Cap
- Poisonous ☹
- Flattened top
- White cap with brownish scales
- Gills are free and white, turning green as they mature

False Morel
- Poisonous ☹
- Red-brown cap - irregularly lobed, like a brain
- Tube-like hollows
- Yellowish spore print
- Smooth with more wrinkles as it ages

Destroying Angel
- Poisonous ☹
- White stalk and gills
- White cap or white edge and yellowish, pinkish, or tan center
- Egg-shaped cap

Common Conecap
- Poisonous ☹
- Rust-colored brown gills and conical cap
- Surface smooth, dry
- Adnexed gills
- Slender straight stem
- Brown spore print

Deadly Galerina
- Poisonous ☹
- Brownish, sticky cap, yellowish to rusty gills, ring on stalk
- Edges are curved against gills
- Gills narrow, crowded

Lobster Mushroom
- Edible ☺
- Bumpy, reddish-orange exterior
- Fish-like taste
- Irregular shape with little to no stem
- Cracked cap

King Bolete
- Edible ☺
- Light brown to reddish brown
- Stem very thick and club shaped
- White closely spaced small pores
- White flesh

Spore Print

Notes

_____
_____
_____
_____
_____

Location

Site / GPS: _____ Date: _____

○ Living Tree ○ Leaf Litter ○ Mulch ○ Dead Tree or Wood ○ Grass
○ Soil ○ Other _____

Type of Tree(s) On or Near: _____

Forest Type: ○ Deciduous ○ Coniferous ○ Tropical ○ Other _____

Weather Conditions: _____

General

Size (overall height): _____ Color: _____ Spore Color: _____

Texture: ○ Tough ○ Brittle ○ Leathery ○ Woody ○ Soft ○ Slimy
○ Spongy ○ Powdery ○ Waxy ○ Rubbery ○ Watery (Other) _____

Bruising When Touched? ○ Yes ○ No Notes: _____

Structures: ○ Cup ○ Ring ○ Warts

Cap Characteristics

Campanulate (bell-shaped)

Conical (triangular)

Cylindrical (shaped like half an egg)

Convex (outwardly rounded)

Flat (with top of uniform height)

Infundibuliform (deeply, depressed, funnel-shaped)

Depressed (with a low central region)

Umbonate (with a central bump or knob)

Surface Markings (warts, scales, slime, etc.): _____

Cap Margin: Smooth, Inrolled, Sinuous/Wavy, Other: _____

Color Changes: _____

Undercap

Gills ○
Attachment: Free or Decurrent
Spacing: Crowded, Close, Distant, Subdistant
Color/Bruising: _____

Pores ○
Color: _____
Pore Size: _____
Pore Pattern: _____

Teeth ○
Color: _____
Teeth Length: _____
Flesh: Soft or Tough

Gill Attachment

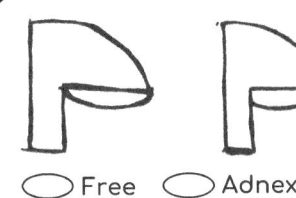

- Free (gills not attached to stem)
- Adnexed (gills attached narrowly to stem)
- Sinuate (gills smoothly notched and running briefly down stem)
- Adnate (gills widely attached widely to stem)
- Descending (gills running down stem for some length)

Stem Shape

   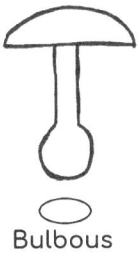 

Tapering — Equal — Club-Shaped — Bulbous — Cup (volva)

Common Mushrooms

Chanterelle
- Edible ☺
- Shape looks like bell of a trumpet
- Bright yellow/orange
- Similar look to Jack o'Lantern

Milk Mushroom
- Edible ☺
- Rounded caps that connect to an elongated, thick stem
- Smooth firm cap
- Color is pure white

Morels
- Edible ☺
- Honeycombed cap
- Most morels cap is longer than stem
- Spore print is usually light colored
- Interior is hollow

Porcini
- Edible ☺
- Large size
- Also known as king bolete
- Resembles reddish/brown hamburger bun

Shaggy Mane
- Edible ☺
- White shaggy cylindrical cap that turns black and inky with age
- Bell shape - mature
- Spore print is black

Death Cap
- Poisonous ☹
- Flattened top
- White cap with brownish scales
- Gills are free and white, turning green as they mature

False Morel
- Poisonous ☹
- Red-brown cap - irregularly lobed, like a brain
- Tube-like hollows
- Yellowish spore print
- Smooth with more wrinkles as it ages

Destroying Angel
- Poisonous ☹
- White stalk and gills
- White cap or white edge and yellowish, pinkish, or tan center
- Egg-shaped cap

Common Conecap
- Poisonous ☹
- Rust-colored brown gills and conical cap
- Surface smooth, dry
- Adnexed gills
- Slender straight stem
- Brown spore print

Deadly Galerina
- Poisonous ☹
- Brownish, sticky cap, yellowish to rusty gills, ring on stalk
- Edges are curved against gills
- Gills narrow, crowded

Lobster Mushroom
- Edible ☺
- Bumpy, reddish-orange exterior
- Fish-like taste
- Irregular shape with little to no stem
- Cracked cap

King Bolete
- Edible ☺
- Light brown to reddish brown
- Stem very thick and club shaped
- White closely spaced small pores
- White flesh

Spore Print

Notes

Location

Site / GPS: _____ Date: _____

○ Living Tree ○ Leaf Litter ○ Mulch ○ Dead Tree or Wood ○ Grass
○ Soil ○ Other _____

Type of Tree(s) On or Near: _____

Forest Type: ○ Deciduous ○ Coniferous ○ Tropical ○ Other _____

Weather Conditions: _____

General

Size (overall height): _____ Color: _____ Spore Color: _____

Texture: ○ Tough ○ Brittle ○ Leathery ○ Woody ○ Soft ○ Slimy
○ Spongy ○ Powdery ○ Waxy ○ Rubbery ○ Watery (Other) _____

Bruising When Touched? ○ Yes ○ No   Notes: _____

Structures: ○ Cup ○ Ring ○ Warts   _____

Cap Characteristics

Campanulate (bell-shaped)

Conical (triangular)

Cylindrical (shaped like half an egg)

Convex (outwardly rounded)

Flat (with top of uniform height)

Infundibuliform (deeply, depressed, funnel-shaped)

Depressed (with a low central region)

Umbonate (with a central bump or knob)

Surface Markings (warts, scales, slime, etc.): _____

Cap Margin: Smooth, Inrolled, Sinuous/Wavy, Other: _____

Color Changes: _____

Undercap

Gills ○
Attachment: Free or Decurrent
Spacing: Crowded, Close, Distant, Subdistant
Color/Bruising: _____

Pores ○
Color: _____
Pore Size: _____
Pore Pattern: _____

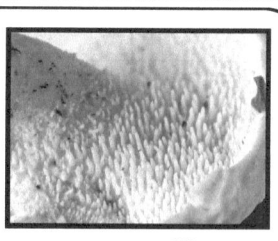

Teeth ○
Color: _____
Teeth Length: _____
Flesh: Soft or Tough

Gill Attachment

○ Free
(gills not attached to stem)

○ Adnexed
(gills attached narrowly to stem)

○ Sinuate
(gills smoothly notched and running briefly down stem)

○ Adnate
(gills widely attached widely to stem)

○ Descenting
(gills running down stem for some length)

Stem Shape

    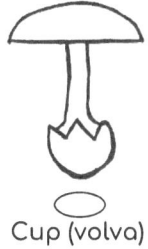

○ Tapering ○ Equal ○ Club-Shaped ○ Bulbous ○ Cup (volva)

Common Mushrooms

Chanterelle
- Edible ☺
- Shape looks like bell of a trumpet
- Bright yellow/orange
- Similar look to Jack o'Lantern

Milk Mushroom
- Edible ☺
- Rounded caps that connect to an elongated, thick stem
- Smooth firm cap
- Color is pure white

Morels
- Edible ☺
- Honeycombed cap
- Most morels cap is longer than stem
- Spore print is usually light colored
- Interior is hollow

Porcini
- Edible ☺
- Large size
- Also known as king bolete
- Resembles reddish/brown hamburger bun

Shaggy Mane
- Edible ☺
- White shaggy cylindrical cap that turns black and inky with age
- Bell shape - mature
- Spore print is black

Death Cap
- Poisonous ☹
- Flattened top
- White cap with brownish scales
- Gills are free and white, turning green as they mature

False Morel
- Poisonous ☹
- Red-brown cap - irregularly lobed, like a brain
- Tube-like hollows
- Yellowish spore print
- Smooth with more wrinkles as it ages

Destroying Angel
- Poisonous ☹
- White stalk and gills
- White cap or white edge and yellowish, pinkish, or tan center
- Egg-shaped cap

Common Conecap
- Poisonous ☹
- Rust-colored brown gills and conical cap
- Surface smooth, dry
- Adnexed gills
- Slender straight stem
- Brown spore print

Deadly Galerina
- Poisonous ☹
- Brownish, sticky cap, yellowish to rusty gills, ring on stalk
- Edges are curved against gills
- Gills narrow, crowded

Lobster Mushroom
- Edible ☺
- Bumpy, reddish-orange exterior
- Fish-like taste
- Irregular shape with little to no stem
- Cracked cap

King Bolete
- Edible ☺
- Light brown to reddish brown
- Stem very thick and club shaped
- White closely spaced small pores
- White flesh

Spore Print

Notes

Location

Site / GPS: _____ Date: _____

○ Living Tree ○ Leaf Litter ○ Mulch ○ Dead Tree or Wood ○ Grass
○ Soil ○ Other _____

Type of Tree(s) On or Near: _____

Forest Type: ○ Deciduous ○ Coniferous ○ Tropical ○ Other _____

Weather Conditions: _____

General

Size (overall height): _____ Color: _____ Spore Color: _____

Texture: ○ Tough ○ Brittle ○ Leathery ○ Woody ○ Soft ○ Slimy
○ Spongy ○ Powdery ○ Waxy ○ Rubbery ○ Watery (Other) _____

Bruising When Touched? ○ Yes ○ No Notes: _____

Structures: ○ Cup ○ Ring ○ Warts _____

Cap Characteristics

Campanulate (bell-shaped)
Conical (triangular)
Cylindrical (shaped like half an egg)
Convex (outwardly rounded)
Flat (with top of uniform height)
Infundibuliform (deeply, depressed, funnel-shaped)
Depressed (with a low central region)
Umbonate (with a central bump or knob)

Surface Markings (warts, scales, slime, etc.): _____

Cap Margin: Smooth, Inrolled, Sinuous/Wavy, Other: _____

Color Changes: _____

Undercap

Gills ○
Attachment: Free or Decurrent
Spacing: Crowded, Close, Distant, Subdistant
Color/Bruising: _____

Pores ○
Color: _____
Pore Size: _____
Pore Pattern: _____

Teeth ○
Color: _____
Teeth Length: _____
Flesh: Soft or Tough

Gill Attachment

 ○ Free
(gills not attached to stem)

 ○ Adnexed
(gills attached narrowly to stem)

 ○ Sinuate
(gills smoothly notched and running briefly down stem)

 ○ Adnate
(gills widely attached widely to stem)

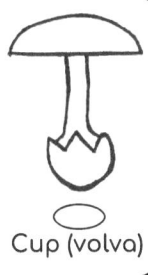 ○ Descending
(gills running down stem for some length)

Stem Shape

- Tapering
- Equal
- Club-Shaped
- Bulbous
- Cup (volva)

Common Mushrooms

Chanterelle
- Edible ☺
- Shape looks like bell of a trumpet
- Bright yellow/orange
- Similar look to Jack o'Lantern

Shaggy Mane
- Edible ☺
- White shaggy cylindrical cap that turns black and inky with age
- Bell shape - mature
- Spore print is black

Common Conecap
- Poisonous ☹
- Rust-colored brown gills and conical cap
- Surface smooth, dry
- Adnexed gills
- Slender straight stem
- Brown spore print

Milk Mushroom
- Edible ☺
- Rounded caps that connect to an elongated, thick stem
- Smooth firm cap
- Color is pure white

Death Cap
- Poisonous ☹
- Flattened top
- White cap with brownish scales
- Gills are free and white, turning green as they mature

Deadly Galerina
- Poisonous ☹
- Brownish, sticky cap, yellowish to rusty gills, ring on stalk
- Edges are curved against gills
- Gills narrow, crowded

Morels
- Edible ☺
- Honeycombed cap
- Most morels cap is longer than stem
- Spore print is usually light colored
- Interior is hollow

False Morel
- Poisonous ☹
- Red-brown cap - irregularly lobed, like a brain
- Tube-like hollows
- Yellowish spore print
- Smooth with more wrinkles as it ages

Lobster Mushroom
- Edible ☺
- Bumpy, reddish-orange exterior
- Fish-like taste
- Irregular shape with little to no stem
- Cracked cap

Porcini
- Edible ☺
- Large size
- Also known as king bolete
- Resembles reddish/brown hamburger bun

Destroying Angel
- Poisonous ☹
- White stalk and gills
- White cap or white edge and yellowish, pinkish, or tan center
- Egg-shaped cap

King Bolete
- Edible ☺
- Light brown to reddish brown
- Stem very thick and club shaped
- White closely spaced small pores
- White flesh

Notes

Spore Print

_____
_____
_____
_____
_____
_____

Location

Site / GPS: _____ Date: _____

○ Living Tree ○ Leaf Litter ○ Mulch ○ Dead Tree or Wood ○ Grass
○ Soil ○ Other _____

Type of Tree(s) On or Near: _____

Forest Type: ○ Deciduous ○ Coniferous ○ Tropical ○ Other _____

Weather Conditions: _____

General

Size (overall height): _____ Color: _____ Spore Color: _____

Texture: ○ Tough ○ Brittle ○ Leathery ○ Woody ○ Soft ○ Slimy
○ Spongy ○ Powdery ○ Waxy ○ Rubbery ○ Watery (Other) _____

Bruising When Touched? ○ Yes ○ No   Notes: _____

Structures: ○ Cup ○ Ring ○ Warts   _____

Cap Characteristics

Campanulate (bell-shaped)

Conical (triangular)

Cylindrical (shaped like half an egg)

Convex (outwardly rounded)

Flat (with top of uniform height)

Infundibuliform (deeply, depressed, funnel-shaped)

Depressed (with a low central region)

Umbonate (with a central bump or knob)

Surface Markings (warts, scales, slime, etc.): _____

Cap Margin: Smooth, Inrolled, Sinuous/Wavy, Other: _____

Color Changes: _____

Undercap

Gills ○
Attachment: Free or Decurrent
Spacing: Crowded, Close, Distant, Subdistant
Color/Bruising: _____

Pores ○
Color: _____
Pore Size: _____
Pore Pattern: _____

Teeth ○
Color: _____
Teeth Length: _____
Flesh: Soft or Tough

Gill Attachment

- Free (gills not attached to stem)
- Adnexed (gills attached narrowly to stem)
- Sinuate (gills smoothly notched and running briefly down stem)
- Adnate (gills widely attached widely to stem)
- Descenting (gills running down stem for some length)

Stem Shape

 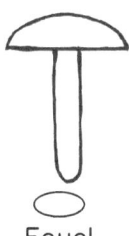   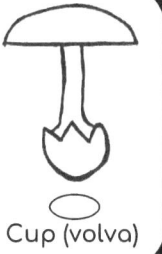

- Tapering
- Equal
- Club-Shaped
- Bulbous
- Cup (volva)

Common Mushrooms

Chanterelle
- Edible ☺
- Shape looks like bell of a trumpet
- Bright yellow/orange
- Similar look to Jack o'Lantern

Shaggy Mane
- Edible ☺
- White shaggy cylindrical cap that turns black and inky with age
- Bell shape - mature
- Spore print is black

Common Conecap
- Poisonous ☹
- Rust-colored brown gills and conical cap
- Surface smooth, dry
- Adnexed gills
- Slender straight stem
- Brown spore print

Milk Mushroom
- Edible ☺
- Rounded caps that connect to an elongated, thick stem
- Smooth firm cap
- Color is pure white

Death Cap
- Poisonous ☹
- Flattened top
- White cap with brownish scales
- Gills are free and white, turning green as they mature

Deadly Galerina
- Poisonous ☹
- Brownish, sticky cap, yellowish to rusty gills, ring on stalk
- Edges are curved against gills
- Gills narrow, crowded

Morels
- Edible ☺
- Honeycombed cap
- Most morels cap is longer than stem
- Spore print is usually light colored
- Interior is hollow

False Morel
- Poisonous ☹
- Red-brown cap - irregularly lobed, like a brain
- Tube-like hollows
- Yellowish spore print
- Smooth with more wrinkles as it ages

Lobster Mushroom
- Edible ☺
- Bumpy, reddish-orange exterior
- Fish-like taste
- Irregular shape with little to no stem
- Cracked cap

Porcini
- Edible ☺
- Large size
- Also known as king bolete
- Resembles reddish/brown hamburger bun

Destroying Angel
- Poisonous ☹
- White stalk and gills
- White cap or white edge and yellowish, pinkish, or tan center
- Egg-shaped cap

King Bolete
- Edible ☺
- Light brown to reddish brown
- Stem very thick and club shaped
- White closely spaced small pores
- White flesh

Spore Print

Notes

Location

Site / GPS: _____ Date: _____

○ Living Tree ○ Leaf Litter ○ Mulch ○ Dead Tree or Wood ○ Grass
○ Soil ○ Other _____

Type of Tree(s) On or Near: _____

Forest Type: ○ Deciduous ○ Coniferous ○ Tropical ○ Other _____

Weather Conditions: _____

General

Size (overall height): _____ Color: _____ Spore Color: _____

Texture: ○ Tough ○ Brittle ○ Leathery ○ Woody ○ Soft ○ Slimy
○ Spongy ○ Powdery ○ Waxy ○ Rubbery ○ Watery (Other) _____

Bruising When Touched? ○ Yes ○ No   Notes: _____

Structures: ○ Cup ○ Ring ○ Warts   _____

Cap Characteristics

Campanulate (bell-shaped)

Conical (triangular)

Cylindrical (shaped like half an egg)

Convex (outwardly rounded)

Flat (with top of uniform height)

Infundibuliform (deeply, depressed, funnel-shaped)

Depressed (with a low central region)

Umbonate (with a central bump or knob)

Surface Markings (warts, scales, slime, etc.): _____

Cap Margin: Smooth, Inrolled, Sinuous/Wavy, Other: _____

Color Changes: _____

Undercap

Gills ○
Attachment: Free or Decurrent
Spacing: Crowded, Close, Distant, Subdistant
Color/Bruising: _____

Pores ○
Color: _____
Pore Size: _____
Pore Pattern: _____

Teeth ○
Color: _____
Teeth Length: _____
Flesh: Soft or Tough

Gill Attachment

○ Free
(gills not attached to stem)

○ Adnexed
(gills attached narrowly to stem)

○ Sinuate
(gills smoothly notched and running briefly down stem)

○ Adnate
(gills widely attached widely to stem)

○ Descending
(gills running down stem for some length)

Stem Shape

Tapering Equal Club-Shaped Bulbous Cup (volva)

Common Mushrooms

Chanterelle

- Edible ☺
- Shape looks like bell of a trumpet
- Bright yellow/orange
- Similar look to Jack o'Lantern

Shaggy Mane
- Edible ☺
- White shaggy cylindrical cap that turns black and inky with age
- Bell shape - mature
- Spore print is black

Common Conecap
- Poisonous ☹
- Rust-colored brown gills and conical cap
- Surface smooth, dry
- Adnexed gills
- Slender straight stem
- Brown spore print

Milk Mushroom
- Edible ☺
- Rounded caps that connect to an elongated, thick stem
- Smooth firm cap
- Color is pure white

Death Cap
- Poisonous ☹
- Flattened top
- White cap with brownish scales
- Gills are free and white, turning green as they mature

Deadly Galerina
- Poisonous ☹
- Brownish, sticky cap, yellowish to rusty gills, ring on stalk
- Edges are curved against gills
- Gills narrow, crowded

Morels

- Edible ☺
- Honeycombed cap
- Most morels cap is longer than stem
- Spore print is usually light colored
- Interior is hollow

False Morel
- Poisonous ☹
- Red-brown cap - irregularly lobed, like a brain
- Tube-like hollows
- Yellowish spore print
- Smooth with more wrinkles as it ages

Lobster Mushroom
- Edible ☺
- Bumpy, reddish-orange exterior
- Fish-like taste
- Irregular shape with little to no stem
- Cracked cap

Porcini

- Edible ☺
- Large size
- Also known as king bolete
- Resembles reddish/brown hamburger bun

Destroying Angel
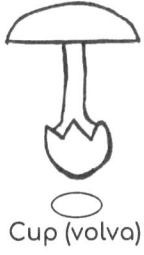
- Poisonous ☹
- White stalk and gills
- White cap or white edge and yellowish, pinkish, or tan center
- Egg-shaped cap

King Bolete
- Edible ☺
- Light brown to reddish brown
- Stem very thick and club shaped
- White closely spaced small pores
- White flesh

Spore Print

_____
_____
_____
_____
_____
_____

Notes

Location

Site / GPS: _____ Date: _____

○ Living Tree ○ Leaf Litter ○ Mulch ○ Dead Tree or Wood ○ Grass
○ Soil ○ Other _____

Type of Tree(s) On or Near: _____

Forest Type: ○ Deciduous ○ Coniferous ○ Tropical ○ Other _____

Weather Conditions: _____

General

Size (overall height): _____ Color: _____ Spore Color: _____

Texture: ○ Tough ○ Brittle ○ Leathery ○ Woody ○ Soft ○ Slimy
○ Spongy ○ Powdery ○ Waxy ○ Rubbery ○ Watery (Other) _____

Bruising When Touched? ○ Yes ○ No   Notes: _____

Structures: ○ Cup ○ Ring ○ Warts

Cap Characteristics

Campanulate (bell-shaped)

Conical (triangular)

Cylindrical (shaped like half an egg)

Convex (outwardly rounded)

Flat (with top of uniform height)

Infundibuliform (deeply, depressed, funnel-shaped)

Depressed (with a low central region)

Umbonate (with a central bump or knob)

Surface Markings (warts, scales, slime, etc.): _____

Cap Margin: Smooth, Inrolled, Sinuous/Wavy, Other: _____

Color Changes: _____

Undercap

Gills ○
Attachment: Free or Decurrent
Spacing: Crowded, Close, Distant, Subdistant
Color/Bruising: _____

Pores ○
Color: _____
Pore Size: _____
Pore Pattern: _____

Teeth ○
Color: _____
Teeth Length: _____
Flesh: Soft or Tough

Gill Attachment

  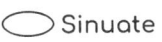  

○ Free	○ Adnexed	○ Sinuate	○ Adnate	○ Descending
(gills not attached to stem)	(gills attached narrowly to stem)	(gills smoothly notched and running briefly down stem)	(gills widely attached widely to stem)	(gills running down stem for some length)

Stem Shape

    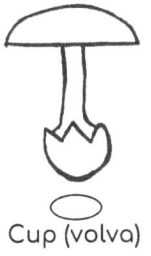

○ Tapering   ○ Equal   ○ Club-Shaped   ○ Bulbous   ○ Cup (volva)

Common Mushrooms

Chanterelle
- Edible ☺
- Shape looks like bell of a trumpet
- Bright yellow/orange
- Similar look to Jack o'Lantern

Milk Mushroom
- Edible ☺
- Rounded caps that connect to an elongated, thick stem
- Smooth firm cap
- Color is pure white

Morels
- Edible ☺
- Honeycombed cap
- Most morels cap is longer than stem
- Spore print is usually light colored
- Interior is hollow

Porcini
- Edible ☺
- Large size
- Also known as king bolete
- Resembles reddish/brown hamburger bun

Shaggy Mane
- Edible ☺
- White shaggy cylindrical cap that turns black and inky with age
- Bell shape - mature
- Spore print is black

Death Cap
- Poisonous ☹
- Flattened top
- White cap with brownish scales
- Gills are free and white, turning green as they mature

False Morel
- Poisonous ☹
- Red-brown cap - irregularly lobed, like a brain
- Tube-like hollows
- Yellowish spore print
- Smooth with more wrinkles as it ages

Destroying Angel
- Poisonous ☹
- White stalk and gills
- White cap or white edge and yellowish, pinkish, or tan center
- Egg-shaped cap

Common Conecap
- Poisonous ☹
- Rust-colored brown gills and conical cap
- Surface smooth, dry
- Adnexed gills
- Slender straight stem
- Brown spore print

Deadly Galerina
- Poisonous ☹
- Brownish, sticky cap, yellowish to rusty gills, ring on stalk
- Edges are curved against gills
- Gills narrow, crowded

Lobster Mushroom
- Edible ☺
- Bumpy, reddish-orange exterior
- Fish-like taste
- Irregular shape with little to no stem
- Cracked cap

King Bolete
- Edible ☺
- Light brown to reddish brown
- Stem very thick and club shaped
- White closely spaced small pores
- White flesh

Spore Print

Notes

_____
_____
_____
_____
_____
_____

Location

Site / GPS: _____ Date: _____

○ Living Tree ○ Leaf Litter ○ Mulch ○ Dead Tree or Wood ○ Grass
○ Soil ○ Other _____

Type of Tree(s) On or Near: _____

Forest Type: ○ Deciduous ○ Coniferous ○ Tropical ○ Other _____

Weather Conditions: _____

General

Size (overall height): _____ Color: _____ Spore Color: _____

Texture: ○ Tough ○ Brittle ○ Leathery ○ Woody ○ Soft ○ Slimy
○ Spongy ○ Powdery ○ Waxy ○ Rubbery ○ Watery (Other) _____

Bruising When Touched? ○ Yes ○ No   Notes: _____

Structures: ○ Cup ○ Ring ○ Warts   _____

Cap Characteristics

Campanulate (bell-shaped)

Conical (triangular)

Cylindrical (shaped like half an egg)

Convex (outwardly rounded)

Flat (with top of uniform height)

Infundibuliform (deeply, depressed, funnel-shaped)

Depressed (with a low central region)

Umbonate (with a central bump or knob)

Surface Markings (warts, scales, slime, etc.): _____

Cap Margin: Smooth, Inrolled, Sinuous/Wavy, Other: _____

Color Changes: _____

Undercap

Gills ○
Attachment: Free or Decurrent
Spacing: Crowded, Close, Distant, Subdistant
Color/Bruising: _____

Pores ○
Color: _____
Pore Size: _____
Pore Pattern: _____

Teeth ○
Color: _____
Teeth Length: _____
Flesh: Soft or Tough

Gill Attachment

- **Free** (gills not attached to stem)
- **Adnexed** (gills attached narrowly to stem)
- **Sinuate** (gills smoothly notched and running briefly down stem)
- **Adnate** (gills widely attached widely to stem)
- **Descenting** (gills running down stem for some length)

Stem Shape

    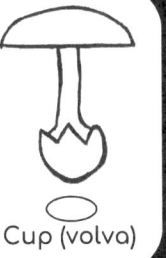

- Tapering
- Equal
- Club-Shaped
- Bulbous
- Cup (volva)

Common Mushrooms

Chanterelle
- Edible ☺
- Shape looks like bell of a trumpet
- Bright yellow/orange
- Similar look to Jack o'Lantern

Milk Mushroom
- Edible ☺
- Rounded caps that connect to an elongated, thick stem
- Smooth firm cap
- Color is pure white

Morels
- Edible ☺
- Honeycombed cap
- Most morels cap is longer than stem
- Spore print is usually light colored
- Interior is hollow

Porcini
- Edible ☺
- Large size
- Also known as king bolete
- Resembles reddish/brown hamburger bun

Shaggy Mane
- Edible ☺
- White shaggy cylindrical cap that turns black and inky with age
- Bell shape - mature
- Spore print is black

Death Cap
- Poisonous ☹
- Flattened top
- White cap with brownish scales
- Gills are free and white, turning green as they mature

False Morel
- Poisonous ☹
- Red-brown cap - irregularly lobed, like a brain
- Tube-like hollows
- Yellowish spore print
- Smooth with more wrinkles as it ages

Destroying Angel
- Poisonous ☹
- White stalk and gills
- White cap or white edge and yellowish, pinkish, or tan center
- Egg-shaped cap

Common Conecap
- Poisonous ☹
- Rust-colored brown gills and conical cap
- Surface smooth, dry
- Adnexed gills
- Slender straight stem
- Brown spore print

Deadly Galerina
- Poisonous ☹
- Brownish, sticky cap, yellowish to rusty gills, ring on stalk
- Edges are curved against gills
- Gills narrow, crowded

Lobster Mushroom
- Edible ☺
- Bumpy, reddish-orange exterior
- Fish-like taste
- Irregular shape with little to no stem
- Cracked cap

King Bolete
- Edible ☺
- Light brown to reddish brown
- Stem very thick and club shaped
- White closely spaced small pores
- White flesh

Spore Print

Notes

_____
_____
_____
_____
_____
_____

Location

Site / GPS: _____ Date: _____

○ Living Tree ○ Leaf Litter ○ Mulch ○ Dead Tree or Wood ○ Grass
○ Soil ○ Other _____

Type of Tree(s) On or Near: _____

Forest Type: ○ Deciduous ○ Coniferous ○ Tropical ○ Other _____

Weather Conditions: _____

General

Size (overall height): _____ Color: _____ Spore Color: _____

Texture: ○ Tough ○ Brittle ○ Leathery ○ Woody ○ Soft ○ Slimy
○ Spongy ○ Powdery ○ Waxy ○ Rubbery ○ Watery (Other) _____

Bruising When Touched? ○ Yes ○ No   Notes: _____

Structures: ○ Cup ○ Ring ○ Warts

Cap Characteristics

Campanulate (bell-shaped)

Conical (triangular)

Cylindrical (shaped like half an egg)

Convex (outwardly rounded)

Flat (with top of uniform height)

Infundibuliform (deeply, depressed, funnel-shaped)

Depressed (with a low central region)

Umbonate (with a central bump or knob)

Surface Markings (warts, scales, slime, etc.): _____

Cap Margin: Smooth, Inrolled, Sinuous/Wavy, Other: _____

Color Changes: _____

Undercap

Gills ○
Attachment: Free or Decurrent
Spacing: Crowded, Close, Distant, Subdistant
Color/Bruising: _____

Pores ○
Color: _____
Pore Size: _____
Pore Pattern: _____

Teeth ○
Color: _____
Teeth Length: _____
Flesh: Soft or Tough

Gill Attachment

○ Free
(gills not attached to stem)

○ Adnexed
(gills attached narrowly to stem)

○ Sinuate
(gills smoothly notched and running briefly down stem)

○ Adnate
(gills widely attached widely to stem)

○ Descending
(gills running down stem for some length)

Stem Shape

 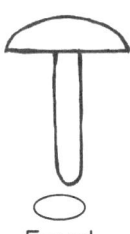   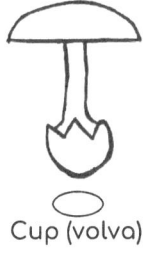

Tapering — Equal — Club-Shaped — Bulbous — Cup (volva)

Common Mushrooms

Chanterelle
- Edible ☺
- Shape looks like bell of a trumpet
- Bright yellow/orange
- Similar look to Jack o'Lantern

Shaggy Mane
- Edible ☺
- White shaggy cylindrical cap that turns black and inky with age
- Bell shape - mature
- Spore print is black

Common Conecap
- Poisonous ☹
- Rust-colored brown gills and conical cap
- Surface smooth, dry
- Adnexed gills
- Slender straight stem
- Brown spore print

Milk Mushroom
- Edible ☺
- Rounded caps that connect to an elongated, thick stem
- Smooth firm cap
- Color is pure white

Death Cap
- Poisonous ☹
- Flattened top
- White cap with brownish scales
- Gills are free and white, turning green as they mature

Deadly Galerina
- Poisonous ☹
- Brownish, sticky cap, yellowish to rusty gills, ring on stalk
- Edges are curved against gills
- Gills narrow, crowded

Morels
- Edible ☺
- Honeycombed cap
- Most morels cap is longer than stem
- Spore print is usually light colored
- Interior is hollow

False Morel
- Poisonous ☹
- Red-brown cap - irregularly lobed, like a brain
- Tube-like hollows
- Yellowish spore print
- Smooth with more wrinkles as it ages

Lobster Mushroom
- Edible ☺
- Bumpy, reddish-orange exterior
- Fish-like taste
- Irregular shape with little to no stem
- Cracked cap

Porcini
- Edible ☺
- Large size
- Also known as king bolete
- Resembles reddish/brown hamburger bun

Destroying Angel
- Poisonous ☹
- White stalk and gills
- White cap or white edge and yellowish, pinkish, or tan center
- Egg-shaped cap

King Bolete
- Edible ☺
- Light brown to reddish brown
- Stem very thick and club shaped
- White closely spaced small pores
- White flesh

Spore Print

Notes

_____
_____
_____
_____
_____

Location

Site / GPS: _____ Date: _____

◯ Living Tree ◯ Leaf Litter ◯ Mulch ◯ Dead Tree or Wood ◯ Grass
◯ Soil ◯ Other _____

Type of Tree(s) On or Near: _____

Forest Type: ◯ Deciduous ◯ Coniferous ◯ Tropical ◯ Other _____

Weather Conditions: _____

General

Size (overall height): _____ Color: _____ Spore Color: _____

Texture: ◯ Tough ◯ Brittle ◯ Leathery ◯ Woody ◯ Soft ◯ Slimy
◯ Spongy ◯ Powdery ◯ Waxy ◯ Rubbery ◯ Watery (Other) _____

Bruising When Touched? ◯ Yes ◯ No   Notes: _____

Structures: ◯ Cup ◯ Ring ◯ Warts   _____

Cap Characteristics

Campanulate (bell-shaped)

Conical (triangular)

Cylindrical (shaped like half an egg)

Convex (outwardly rounded)

Flat (with top of uniform height)

Infundibuliform (deeply, depressed, funnel-shaped)

Depressed (with a low central region)

Umbonate (with a central bump or knob)

Surface Markings (warts, scales, slime, etc.): _____

Cap Margin: Smooth, Inrolled, Sinuous/Wavy, Other: _____

Color Changes: _____

Undercap

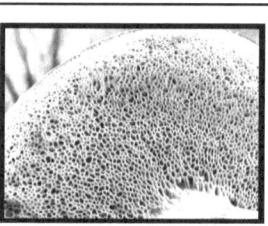

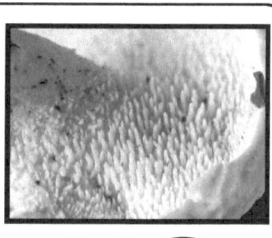

Gills ◯
Attachment: Free or Decurrent
Spacing: Crowded, Close, Distant, Subdistant
Color/Bruising: _____

Pores ◯
Color: _____
Pore Size: _____
Pore Pattern: _____

Teeth ◯
Color: _____
Teeth Length: _____
Flesh: Soft or Tough

Gill Attachment

- Free (gills not attached to stem)
- Adnexed (gills attached narrowly to stem)
- Sinuate (gills smoothly notched and running briefly down stem)
- Adnate (gills widely attached widely to stem)
- Descending (gills running down stem for some length)

Stem Shape

  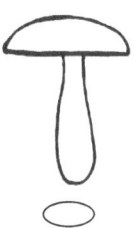  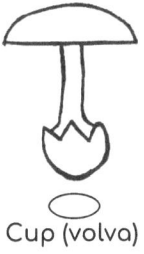

Tapering   Equal   Club-Shaped   Bulbous   Cup (volva)

Common Mushrooms

Chanterelle
- Edible ☺
- Shape looks like bell of a trumpet
- Bright yellow/orange
- Similar look to Jack o'Lantern

Milk Mushroom
- Edible ☺
- Rounded caps that connect to an elongated, thick stem
- Smooth firm cap
- Color is pure white

Morels
- Edible ☺
- Honeycombed cap
- Most morels cap is longer than stem
- Spore print is usually light colored
- Interior is hollow

Porcini
- Edible ☺
- Large size
- Also known as king bolete
- Resembles reddish/brown hamburger bun

Shaggy Mane
- Edible ☺
- White shaggy cylindrical cap that turns black and inky with age
- Bell shape - mature
- Spore print is black

Death Cap
- Poisonous ☹
- Flattened top
- White cap with brownish scales
- Gills are free and white, turning green as they mature

False Morel
- Poisonous ☹
- Red-brown cap - irregularly lobed, like a brain
- Tube-like hollows
- Yellowish spore print
- Smooth with more wrinkles as it ages

Destroying Angel
- Poisonous ☹
- White stalk and gills
- White cap or white edge and yellowish, pinkish, or tan center
- Egg-shaped cap

Common Conecap
- Poisonous ☹
- Rust-colored brown gills and conical cap
- Surface smooth, dry
- Adnexed gills
- Slender straight stem
- Brown spore print

Deadly Galerina
- Poisonous ☹
- Brownish, sticky cap, yellowish to rusty gills, ring on stalk
- Edges are curved against gills
- Gills narrow, crowded

Lobster Mushroom
- Edible ☺
- Bumpy, reddish-orange exterior
- Fish-like taste
- Irregular shape with little to no stem
- Cracked cap

King Bolete
- Edible ☺
- Light brown to reddish brown
- Stem very thick and club shaped
- White closely spaced small pores
- White flesh

Spore Print

Notes

_____

_____

_____

_____

_____

Location

Site / GPS: _____ Date: _____

○ Living Tree ○ Leaf Litter ○ Mulch ○ Dead Tree or Wood ○ Grass
○ Soil ○ Other _____

Type of Tree(s) On or Near: _____

Forest Type: ○ Deciduous ○ Coniferous ○ Tropical ○ Other _____

Weather Conditions: _____

General

Size (overall height): _____ Color: _____ Spore Color: _____

Texture: ○ Tough ○ Brittle ○ Leathery ○ Woody ○ Soft ○ Slimy
○ Spongy ○ Powdery ○ Waxy ○ Rubbery ○ Watery (Other) _____

Bruising When Touched? ○ Yes ○ No   Notes: _____

Structures: ○ Cup ○ Ring ○ Warts   _____

Cap Characteristics

Campanulate (bell-shaped)

Conical (triangular)

Cylindrical (shaped like half an egg)

Convex (outwardly rounded)

Flat (with top of uniform height)

Infundibuliform (deeply, depressed, funnel-shaped)

Depressed (with a low central region)

Umbonate (with a central bump or knob)

Surface Markings (warts, scales, slime, etc.): _____

Cap Margin: Smooth, Inrolled, Sinuous/Wavy, Other: _____

Color Changes: _____

Undercap

Gills ○
Attachment: Free or Decurrent
Spacing: Crowded, Close, Distant, Subdistant
Color/Bruising: _____

Pores ○
Color: _____
Pore Size: _____
Pore Pattern: _____

Teeth ○
Color: _____
Teeth Length: _____
Flesh: Soft or Tough

Gill Attachment

- ○ Free (gills not attached to stem)
- ○ Adnexed (gills attached narrowly to stem)
- ○ Sinuate (gills smoothly notched and running briefly down stem)
- ○ Adnate (gills widely attached widely to stem)
- ○ Descending (gills running down stem for some length)

Stem Shape

 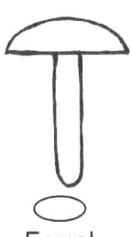  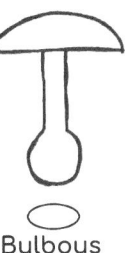 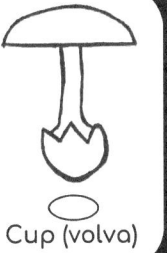

Tapering   Equal   Club-Shaped   Bulbous   Cup (volva)

Common Mushrooms

Chanterelle
- Edible ☺
- Shape looks like bell of a trumpet
- Bright yellow/orange
- Similar look to Jack o'Lantern

Shaggy Mane
- Edible ☺
- White shaggy cylindrical cap that turns black and inky with age
- Bell shape - mature
- Spore print is black

Common Conecap
- Poisonous ☹
- Rust-colored brown gills and conical cap
- Surface smooth, dry
- Adnexed gills
- Slender straight stem
- Brown spore print

Milk Mushroom
- Edible ☺
- Rounded caps that connect to an elongated, thick stem
- Smooth firm cap
- Color is pure white

Death Cap
- Poisonous ☹
- Flattened top
- White cap with brownish scales
- Gills are free and white, turning green as they mature

Deadly Galerina
- Poisonous ☹
- Brownish, sticky cap, yellowish to rusty gills, ring on stalk
- Edges are curved against gills
- Gills narrow, crowded

Morels
- Edible ☺
- Honeycombed cap
- Most morels cap is longer than stem
- Spore print is usually light colored
- Interior is hollow

False Morel
- Poisonous ☹
- Red-brown cap - irregularly lobed, like a brain
- Tube-like hollows
- Yellowish spore print
- Smooth with more wrinkles as it ages

Lobster Mushroom
- Edible ☺
- Bumpy, reddish-orange exterior
- Fish-like taste
- Irregular shape with little to no stem
- Cracked cap

Porcini
- Edible ☺
- Large size
- Also known as king bolete
- Resembles reddish/brown hamburger bun

Destroying Angel
- Poisonous ☹
- White stalk and gills
- White cap or white edge and yellowish, pinkish, or tan center
- Egg-shaped cap

King Bolete
- Edible ☺
- Light brown to reddish brown
- Stem very thick and club shaped
- White closely spaced small pores
- White flesh

Spore Print

Notes

_____
_____
_____
_____
_____
_____

Location

Site / GPS: _____ Date: _____

○ Living Tree ○ Leaf Litter ○ Mulch ○ Dead Tree or Wood ○ Grass
○ Soil ○ Other _____

Type of Tree(s) On or Near: _____

Forest Type: ○ Deciduous ○ Coniferous ○ Tropical ○ Other _____

Weather Conditions: _____

General

Size (overall height): _____ Color: _____ Spore Color: _____

Texture: ○ Tough ○ Brittle ○ Leathery ○ Woody ○ Soft ○ Slimy
○ Spongy ○ Powdery ○ Waxy ○ Rubbery ○ Watery (Other) _____

Bruising When Touched? ○ Yes ○ No   Notes: _____

Structures: ○ Cup ○ Ring ○ Warts

Cap Characteristics

Campanulate (bell-shaped)

Conical (triangular)

Cylindrical (shaped like half an egg)

Convex (outwardly rounded)

Flat (with top of uniform height)

Infundibuliform (deeply, depressed, funnel-shaped)

Depressed (with a low central region)

Umbonate (with a central bump or knob)

Surface Markings (warts, scales, slime, etc.): _____

Cap Margin: Smooth, Inrolled, Sinuous/Wavy, Other: _____

Color Changes: _____

Undercap

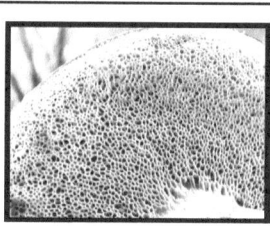
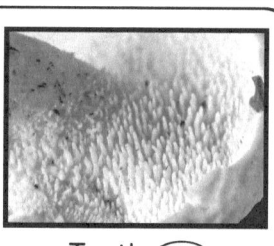

Gills ○

Attachment: Free or Decurrent

Spacing: Crowded, Close, Distant, Subdistant

Color/Bruising: _____

Pores ○

Color: _____

Pore Size: _____

Pore Pattern: _____

Teeth ○

Color: _____

Teeth Length: _____

Flesh: Soft or Tough

Gill Attachment

○ Free
(gills not attached to stem)

○ Adnexed
(gills attached narrowly to stem)

○ Sinuate
(gills smoothly notched and running briefly down stem)

○ Adnate
(gills widely attached widely to stem)

○ Descending
(gills running down stem for some length)

Stem Shape

    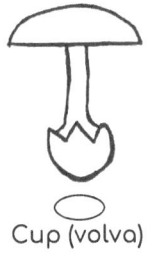

Tapering — Equal — Club-Shaped — Bulbous — Cup (volva)

Common Mushrooms

Chanterelle
- Edible ☺
- Shape looks like bell of a trumpet
- Bright yellow/orange
- Similar look to Jack o'Lantern

Milk Mushroom
- Edible ☺
- Rounded caps that connect to an elongated, thick stem
- Smooth firm cap
- Color is pure white

Morels
- Edible ☺
- Honeycombed cap
- Most morels cap is longer than stem
- Spore print is usually light colored
- Interior is hollow

Porcini
- Edible ☺
- Large size
- Also known as king bolete
- Resembles reddish/brown hamburger bun

Shaggy Mane
- Edible ☺
- White shaggy cylindrical cap that turns black and inky with age
- Bell shape - mature
- Spore print is black

Death Cap
- Poisonous ☹
- Flattened top
- White cap with brownish scales
- Gills are free and white, turning green as they mature

False Morel
- Poisonous ☹
- Red-brown cap - irregularly lobed, like a brain
- Tube-like hollows
- Yellowish spore print
- Smooth with more wrinkles as it ages

Destroying Angel
- Poisonous ☹
- White stalk and gills
- White cap or white edge and yellowish, pinkish, or tan center
- Egg-shaped cap

Common Conecap
- Poisonous ☹
- Rust-colored brown gills and conical cap
- Surface smooth, dry
- Adnexed gills
- Slender straight stem
- Brown spore print

Deadly Galerina
- Poisonous ☹
- Brownish, sticky cap, yellowish to rusty gills, ring on stalk
- Edges are curved against gills
- Gills narrow, crowded

Lobster Mushroom
- Edible ☺
- Bumpy, reddish-orange exterior
- Fish-like taste
- Irregular shape with little to no stem
- Cracked cap

King Bolete
- Edible ☺
- Light brown to reddish brown
- Stem very thick and club shaped
- White closely spaced small pores
- White flesh

Spore Print

Notes

_____
_____
_____
_____
_____

Location

Site / GPS: _____ Date: _____

○ Living Tree ○ Leaf Litter ○ Mulch ○ Dead Tree or Wood ○ Grass
○ Soil ○ Other _____

Type of Tree(s) On or Near: _____

Forest Type: ○ Deciduous ○ Coniferous ○ Tropical ○ Other _____

Weather Conditions: _____

General

Size (overall height): _____ Color: _____ Spore Color: _____

Texture: ○ Tough ○ Brittle ○ Leathery ○ Woody ○ Soft ○ Slimy
○ Spongy ○ Powdery ○ Waxy ○ Rubbery ○ Watery (Other) _____

Bruising When Touched? ○ Yes ○ No   Notes: _____

Structures: ○ Cup ○ Ring ○ Warts

Cap Characteristics

Campanulate (bell-shaped)

Conical (triangular)

Cylindrical (shaped like half an egg)

Convex (outwardly rounded)

Flat (with top of uniform height)

Infundibuliform (deeply, depressed, funnel-shaped)

Depressed (with a low central region)

Umbonate (with a central bump or knob)

Surface Markings (warts, scales, slime, etc.): _____

Cap Margin: Smooth, Inrolled, Sinuous/Wavy, Other: _____

Color Changes: _____

Undercap

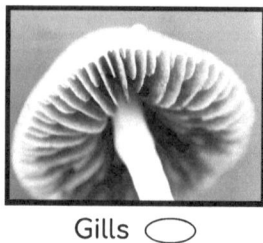

Gills ○
Attachment: Free or Decurrent
Spacing: Crowded, Close, Distant, Subdistant
Color/Bruising: _____

Pores ○
Color: _____
Pore Size: _____
Pore Pattern: _____

Teeth ○
Color: _____
Teeth Length: _____
Flesh: Soft or Tough

Gill Attachment

- ○ Free (gills not attached to stem)
- ○ Adnexed (gills attached narrowly to stem)
- ○ Sinuate (gills smoothly notched and running briefly down stem)
- ○ Adnate (gills widely attached widely to stem)
- ○ Descending (gills running down stem for some length)

Stem Shape

Tapering | Equal | Club-Shaped | Bulbous | Cup (volva)

Common Mushrooms

Chanterelle
- Edible ☺
- Shape looks like bell of a trumpet
- Bright yellow/orange
- Similar look to Jack o'Lantern

Milk Mushroom
- Edible ☺
- Rounded caps that connect to an elongated, thick stem
- Smooth firm cap
- Color is pure white

Morels
- Edible ☺
- Honeycombed cap
- Most morels cap is longer than stem
- Spore print is usually light colored
- Interior is hollow

Porcini
- Edible ☺
- Large size
- Also known as king bolete
- Resembles reddish/brown hamburger bun

Shaggy Mane
- Edible ☺
- White shaggy cylindrical cap that turns black and inky with age
- Bell shape - mature
- Spore print is black

Death Cap
- Poisonous ☹
- Flattened top
- White cap with brownish scales
- Gills are free and white, turning green as they mature

False Morel
- Poisonous ☹
- Red-brown cap - irregularly lobed, like a brain
- Tube-like hollows
- Yellowish spore print
- Smooth with more wrinkles as it ages

Destroying Angel
- Poisonous ☹
- White stalk and gills
- White cap or white edge and yellowish, pinkish, or tan center
- Egg-shaped cap

Common Conecap
- Poisonous ☹
- Rust-colored brown gills and conical cap
- Surface smooth, dry
- Adnexed gills
- Slender straight stem
- Brown spore print

Deadly Galerina
- Poisonous ☹
- Brownish, sticky cap, yellowish to rusty gills, ring on stalk
- Edges are curved against gills
- Gills narrow, crowded

Lobster Mushroom
- Edible ☺
- Bumpy, reddish-orange exterior
- Fish-like taste
- Irregular shape with little to no stem
- Cracked cap

King Bolete
- Edible ☺
- Light brown to reddish brown
- Stem very thick and club shaped
- White closely spaced small pores
- White flesh

Spore Print

Notes

_____
_____
_____
_____
_____
_____

Location

Site / GPS: _____ Date: _____

○ Living Tree ○ Leaf Litter ○ Mulch ○ Dead Tree or Wood ○ Grass
○ Soil ○ Other _____

Type of Tree(s) On or Near: _____

Forest Type: ○ Deciduous ○ Coniferous ○ Tropical ○ Other _____

Weather Conditions: _____

General

Size (overall height): _____ Color: _____ Spore Color: _____

Texture: ○ Tough ○ Brittle ○ Leathery ○ Woody ○ Soft ○ Slimy
○ Spongy ○ Powdery ○ Waxy ○ Rubbery ○ Watery (Other) _____

Bruising When Touched? ○ Yes ○ No   Notes: _____

Structures: ○ Cup ○ Ring ○ Warts

Cap Characteristics

Campanulate (bell-shaped)

Conical (triangular)

Cylindrical (shaped like half an egg)

Convex (outwardly rounded)

Flat (with top of uniform height)

Infundibuliform (deeply, depressed, funnel-shaped)

Depressed (with a low central region)

Umbonate (with a central bump or knob)

Surface Markings (warts, scales, slime, etc.): _____

Cap Margin: Smooth, Inrolled, Sinuous/Wavy, Other: _____

Color Changes: _____

Undercap

Gills ○
Attachment: Free or Decurrent
Spacing: Crowded, Close, Distant, Subdistant
Color/Bruising: _____

Pores ○
Color: _____
Pore Size: _____
Pore Pattern: _____

Teeth ○
Color: _____
Teeth Length: _____
Flesh: Soft or Tough

Gill Attachment

- **Free** (gills not attached to stem)
- **Adnexed** (gills attached narrowly to stem)
- **Sinuate** (gills smoothly notched and running briefly down stem)
- **Adnate** (gills widely attached widely to stem)
- **Descending** (gills running down stem for some length)

Stem Shape

    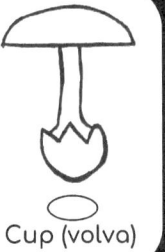

- **Tapering**
- **Equal**
- **Club-Shaped**
- **Bulbous**
- **Cup (volva)**

Common Mushrooms

Chanterelle
- Edible ☺
- Shape looks like bell of a trumpet
- Bright yellow/orange
- Similar look to Jack o'Lantern

Milk Mushroom
- Edible ☺
- Rounded caps that connect to an elongated, thick stem
- Smooth firm cap
- Color is pure white

Morels
- Edible ☺
- Honeycombed cap
- Most morels cap is longer than stem
- Spore print is usually light colored
- Interior is hollow

Porcini
- Edible ☺
- Large size
- Also known as king bolete
- Resembles reddish/brown hamburger bun

Shaggy Mane
- Edible ☺
- White shaggy cylindrical cap that turns black and inky with age
- Bell shape - mature
- Spore print is black

Death Cap
- Poisonous ☹
- Flattened top
- White cap with brownish scales
- Gills are free and white, turning green as they mature

False Morel
- Poisonous ☹
- Red-brown cap - irregularly lobed, like a brain
- Tube-like hollows
- Yellowish spore print
- Smooth with more wrinkles as it ages

Destroying Angel
- Poisonous ☹
- White stalk and gills
- White cap or white edge and yellowish, pinkish, or tan center
- Egg-shaped cap

Common Conecap
- Poisonous ☹
- Rust-colored brown gills and conical cap
- Surface smooth, dry
- Adnexed gills
- Slender straight stem
- Brown spore print

Deadly Galerina
- Poisonous ☹
- Brownish, sticky cap, yellowish to rusty gills, ring on stalk
- Edges are curved against gills
- Gills narrow, crowded

Lobster Mushroom
- Edible ☺
- Bumpy, reddish-orange exterior
- Fish-like taste
- Irregular shape with little to no stem
- Cracked cap

King Bolete
- Edible ☺
- Light brown to reddish brown
- Stem very thick and club shaped
- White closely spaced small pores
- White flesh

Spore Print

_____
_____
_____
_____
_____

Notes

Location

Site / GPS: _____ Date: _____

○ Living Tree ○ Leaf Litter ○ Mulch ○ Dead Tree or Wood ○ Grass
○ Soil ○ Other _____

Type of Tree(s) On or Near: _____

Forest Type: ○ Deciduous ○ Coniferous ○ Tropical ○ Other _____

Weather Conditions: _____

General

Size (overall height): _____ Color: _____ Spore Color: _____

Texture: ○ Tough ○ Brittle ○ Leathery ○ Woody ○ Soft ○ Slimy
○ Spongy ○ Powdery ○ Waxy ○ Rubbery ○ Watery (Other) _____

Bruising When Touched? ○ Yes ○ No   Notes: _____

Structures: ○ Cup ○ Ring ○ Warts

Cap Characteristics

Campanulate (bell-shaped)

Conical (triangular)

Cylindrical (shaped like half an egg)

Convex (outwardly rounded)

Flat (with top of uniform height)

Infundibuliform (deeply, depressed, funnel-shaped)

Depressed (with a low central region)

Umbonate (with a central bump or knob)

Surface Markings (warts, scales, slime, etc.): _____

Cap Margin: Smooth, Inrolled, Sinuous/Wavy, Other: _____

Color Changes: _____

Undercap

Gills ○
Attachment: Free or Decurrent
Spacing: Crowded, Close, Distant, Subdistant
Color/Bruising: _____

Pores ○
Color: _____
Pore Size: _____
Pore Pattern: _____

Teeth ○
Color: _____
Teeth Length: _____
Flesh: Soft or Tough

Gill Attachment

- ○ Free (gills not attached to stem)
- ○ Adnexed (gills attached narrowly to stem)
- ○ Sinuate (gills smoothly notched and running briefly down stem)
- ○ Adnate (gills widely attached widely to stem)
- ○ Descending (gills running down stem for some length)

Stem Shape

    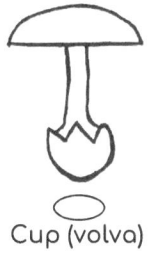

- ○ Tapering
- ○ Equal
- ○ Club-Shaped
- ○ Bulbous
- ○ Cup (volva)

Common Mushrooms

Chanterelle
- Edible ☺
- Shape looks like bell of a trumpet
- Bright yellow/orange
- Similar look to Jack o'Lantern

Milk Mushroom
- Edible ☺
- Rounded caps that connect to an elongated, thick stem
- Smooth firm cap
- Color is pure white

Morels
- Edible ☺
- Honeycombed cap
- Most morels cap is longer than stem
- Spore print is usually light colored
- Interior is hollow

Porcini
- Edible ☺
- Large size
- Also known as king bolete
- Resembles reddish/brown hamburger bun

Shaggy Mane
- Edible ☺
- White shaggy cylindrical cap that turns black and inky with age
- Bell shape - mature
- Spore print is black

Death Cap
- Poisonous ☹
- Flattened top
- White cap with brownish scales
- Gills are free and white, turning green as they mature

False Morel
- Poisonous ☹
- Red-brown cap - irregularly lobed, like a brain
- Tube-like hollows
- Yellowish spore print
- Smooth with more wrinkles as it ages

Destroying Angel
- Poisonous ☹
- White stalk and gills
- White cap or white edge and yellowish, pinkish, or tan center
- Egg-shaped cap

Common Conecap
- Poisonous ☹
- Rust-colored brown gills and conical cap
- Surface smooth, dry
- Adnexed gills
- Slender straight stem
- Brown spore print

Deadly Galerina
- Poisonous ☹
- Brownish, sticky cap, yellowish to rusty gills, ring on stalk
- Edges are curved against gills
- Gills narrow, crowded

Lobster Mushroom
- Edible ☺
- Bumpy, reddish-orange exterior
- Fish-like taste
- Irregular shape with little to no stem
- Cracked cap

King Bolete
- Edible ☺
- Light brown to reddish brown
- Stem very thick and club shaped
- White closely spaced small pores
- White flesh

Spore Print

Notes

Location

Site / GPS: _____ Date: _____

○ Living Tree ○ Leaf Litter ○ Mulch ○ Dead Tree or Wood ○ Grass
○ Soil ○ Other _____

Type of Tree(s) On or Near: _____

Forest Type: ○ Deciduous ○ Coniferous ○ Tropical ○ Other _____

Weather Conditions: _____

General

Size (overall height): _____ Color: _____ Spore Color: _____

Texture: ○ Tough ○ Brittle ○ Leathery ○ Woody ○ Soft ○ Slimy
○ Spongy ○ Powdery ○ Waxy ○ Rubbery ○ Watery (Other) _____

Bruising When Touched? ○ Yes ○ No   Notes: _____

Structures: ○ Cup ○ Ring ○ Warts

Cap Characteristics

Campanulate (bell-shaped)

Conical (triangular)

Cylindrical (shaped like half an egg)

Convex (outwardly rounded)

Flat (with top of uniform height)

Infundibuliform (deeply, depressed, funnel-shaped)

Depressed (with a low central region)

Umbonate (with a central bump or knob)

Surface Markings (warts, scales, slime, etc.): _____

Cap Margin: Smooth, Inrolled, Sinuous/Wavy, Other: _____

Color Changes: _____

Undercap

Gills ○
Attachment: Free or Decurrent
Spacing: Crowded, Close, Distant, Subdistant
Color/Bruising: _____

Pores ○
Color: _____
Pore Size: _____
Pore Pattern: _____

Teeth ○
Color: _____
Teeth Length: _____
Flesh: Soft or Tough

Gill Attachment

- **Free** (gills not attached to stem)
- **Adnexed** (gills attached narrowly to stem)
- **Sinuate** (gills smoothly notched and running briefly down stem)
- **Adnate** (gills widely attached widely to stem)
- **Descending** (gills running down stem for some length)

Stem Shape

    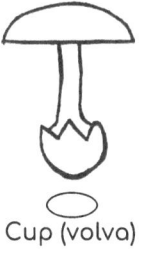

- Tapering
- Equal
- Club-Shaped
- Bulbous
- Cup (volva)

Common Mushrooms

Chanterelle
- Edible ☺
- Shape looks like bell of a trumpet
- Bright yellow/orange
- Similar look to Jack o'Lantern

Shaggy Mane
- Edible ☺
- White shaggy cylindrical cap that turns black and inky with age
- Bell shape - mature
- Spore print is black

Common Conecap
- Poisonous ☹
- Rust-colored brown gills and conical cap
- Surface smooth, dry
- Adnexed gills
- Slender straight stem
- Brown spore print

Milk Mushroom
- Edible ☺
- Rounded caps that connect to an elongated, thick stem
- Smooth firm cap
- Color is pure white

Death Cap
- Poisonous ☹
- Flattened top
- White cap with brownish scales
- Gills are free and white, turning green as they mature

Deadly Galerina
- Poisonous ☹
- Brownish, sticky cap, yellowish to rusty gills, ring on stalk
- Edges are curved against gills
- Gills narrow, crowded

Morels
- Edible ☺
- Honeycombed cap
- Most morels cap is longer than stem
- Spore print is usually light colored
- Interior is hollow

False Morel
- Poisonous ☹
- Red-brown cap - irregularly lobed, like a brain
- Tube-like hollows
- Yellowish spore print
- Smooth with more wrinkles as it ages

Lobster Mushroom
- Edible ☺
- Bumpy, reddish-orange exterior
- Fish-like taste
- Irregular shape with little to no stem
- Cracked cap

Porcini
- Edible ☺
- Large size
- Also known as king bolete
- Resembles reddish/brown hamburger bun

Destroying Angel
- Poisonous ☹
- White stalk and gills
- White cap or white edge and yellowish, pinkish, or tan center
- Egg-shaped cap

King Bolete
- Edible ☺
- Light brown to reddish brown
- Stem very thick and club shaped
- White closely spaced small pores
- White flesh

Spore Print

Notes

_____
_____
_____
_____
_____
_____

Location

Site / GPS: _____ Date: _____

○ Living Tree ○ Leaf Litter ○ Mulch ○ Dead Tree or Wood ○ Grass
○ Soil ○ Other _____

Type of Tree(s) On or Near: _____

Forest Type: ○ Deciduous ○ Coniferous ○ Tropical ○ Other _____

Weather Conditions: _____

General

Size (overall height): _____ Color: _____ Spore Color: _____

Texture: ○ Tough ○ Brittle ○ Leathery ○ Woody ○ Soft ○ Slimy
○ Spongy ○ Powdery ○ Waxy ○ Rubbery ○ Watery (Other) _____

Bruising When Touched? ○ Yes ○ No Notes: _____

Structures: ○ Cup ○ Ring ○ Warts

Cap Characteristics

Campanulate (bell-shaped)

Conical (triangular)

Cylindrical (shaped like half an egg)

Convex (outwardly rounded)

Flat (with top of uniform height)

Infundibuliform (deeply, depressed, funnel-shaped)

Depressed (with a low central region)

Umbonate (with a central bump or knob)

Surface Markings (warts, scales, slime, etc.): _____

Cap Margin: Smooth, Inrolled, Sinuous/Wavy, Other: _____

Color Changes: _____

Undercap

Gills ○
Attachment: Free or Decurrent
Spacing: Crowded, Close, Distant, Subdistant
Color/Bruising: _____

Pores ○
Color: _____
Pore Size: _____
Pore Pattern: _____

Teeth ○
Color: _____
Teeth Length: _____
Flesh: Soft or Tough

Gill Attachment

- ○ Free (gills not attached to stem)
- ○ Adnexed (gills attached narrowly to stem)
- ○ Sinuate (gills smoothly notched and running briefly down stem)
- ○ Adnate (gills widely attached widely to stem)
- ○ Descending (gills running down stem for some length)

Stem Shape

- Tapering
- Equal
- Club-Shaped
- Bulbous
- Cup (volva)

Common Mushrooms

Chanterelle
- Edible ☺
- Shape looks like bell of a trumpet
- Bright yellow/orange
- Similar look to Jack o'Lantern

Shaggy Mane
- Edible ☺
- White shaggy cylindrical cap that turns black and inky with age
- Bell shape - mature
- Spore print is black

Common Conecap
- Poisonous ☹
- Rust-colored brown gills and conical cap
- Surface smooth, dry
- Adnexed gills
- Slender straight stem
- Brown spore print

Milk Mushroom
- Edible ☺
- Rounded caps that connect to an elongated, thick stem
- Smooth firm cap
- Color is pure white

Death Cap
- Poisonous ☹
- Flattened top
- White cap with brownish scales
- Gills are free and white, turning green as they mature

Deadly Galerina
- Poisonous ☹
- Brownish, sticky cap, yellowish to rusty gills, ring on stalk
- Edges are curved against gills
- Gills narrow, crowded

Morels
- Edible ☺
- Honeycombed cap
- Most morels cap is longer than stem
- Spore print is usually light colored
- Interior is hollow

False Morel
- Poisonous ☹
- Red-brown cap - irregularly lobed, like a brain
- Tube-like hollows
- Yellowish spore print
- Smooth with more wrinkles as it ages

Lobster Mushroom
- Edible ☺
- Bumpy, reddish-orange exterior
- Fish-like taste
- Irregular shape with little to no stem
- Cracked cap

Porcini
- Edible ☺
- Large size
- Also known as king bolete
- Resembles reddish/brown hamburger bun

Destroying Angel
- Poisonous ☹
- White stalk and gills
- White cap or white edge and yellowish, pinkish, or tan center
- Egg-shaped cap

King Bolete
- Edible ☺
- Light brown to reddish brown
- Stem very thick and club shaped
- White closely spaced small pores
- White flesh

Spore Print / Notes

_____
_____
_____
_____
_____
_____

Location

Site / GPS: _____ Date: _____

○ Living Tree ○ Leaf Litter ○ Mulch ○ Dead Tree or Wood ○ Grass
○ Soil ○ Other _____

Type of Tree(s) On or Near: _____

Forest Type: ○ Deciduous ○ Coniferous ○ Tropical ○ Other _____

Weather Conditions: _____

General

Size (overall height): _____ Color: _____ Spore Color: _____

Texture: ○ Tough ○ Brittle ○ Leathery ○ Woody ○ Soft ○ Slimy
○ Spongy ○ Powdery ○ Waxy ○ Rubbery ○ Watery (Other) _____

Bruising When Touched? ○ Yes ○ No   Notes: _____

Structures: ○ Cup ○ Ring ○ Warts   _____

Cap Characteristics

Campanulate (bell-shaped)

Conical (triangular)

Cylindrical (shaped like half an egg)

Convex (outwardly rounded)

Flat (with top of uniform height)

Infundibuliform (deeply, depressed, funnel-shaped)

Depressed (with a low central region)

Umbonate (with a central bump or knob)

Surface Markings (warts, scales, slime, etc.): _____

Cap Margin: Smooth, Inrolled, Sinuous/Wavy, Other: _____

Color Changes: _____

Undercap

Gills ○
Attachment: Free or Decurrent
Spacing: Crowded, Close, Distant, Subdistant
Color/Bruising: _____

Pores ○
Color: _____
Pore Size: _____
Pore Pattern: _____

Teeth ○
Color: _____
Teeth Length: _____
Flesh: Soft or Tough

Gill Attachment

- ○ Free (gills not attached to stem)
- ○ Adnexed (gills attached narrowly to stem)
- ○ Sinuate (gills smoothly notched and running briefly down stem)
- ○ Adnate (gills widely attached widely to stem)
- ○ Descending (gills running down stem for some length)

Stem Shape

- Tapering
- Equal
- Club-Shaped
- Bulbous
- Cup (volva)

Common Mushrooms

Chanterelle
- Edible ☺
- Shape looks like bell of a trumpet
- Bright yellow/orange
- Similar look to Jack o'Lantern

Milk Mushroom
- Edible ☺
- Rounded caps that connect to an elongated, thick stem
- Smooth firm cap
- Color is pure white

Morels
- Edible ☺
- Honeycombed cap
- Most morels cap is longer than stem
- Spore print is usually light colored
- Interior is hollow

Porcini
- Edible ☺
- Large size
- Also known as king bolete
- Resembles reddish/brown hamburger bun

Shaggy Mane
- Edible ☺
- White shaggy cylindrical cap that turns black and inky with age
- Bell shape - mature
- Spore print is black

Death Cap
- Poisonous ☹
- Flattened top
- White cap with brownish scales
- Gills are free and white, turning green as they mature

False Morel
- Poisonous ☹
- Red-brown cap - irregularly lobed, like a brain
- Tube-like hollows
- Yellowish spore print
- Smooth with more wrinkles as it ages

Destroying Angel
- Poisonous ☹
- White stalk and gills
- White cap or white edge and yellowish, pinkish, or tan center
- Egg-shaped cap

Common Conecap
- Poisonous ☹
- Rust-colored brown gills and conical cap
- Surface smooth, dry
- Adnexed gills
- Slender straight stem
- Brown spore print

Deadly Galerina
- Poisonous ☹
- Brownish, sticky cap, yellowish to rusty gills, ring on stalk
- Edges are curved against gills
- Gills narrow, crowded

Lobster Mushroom
- Edible ☺
- Bumpy, reddish-orange exterior
- Fish-like taste
- Irregular shape with little to no stem
- Cracked cap

King Bolete
- Edible ☺
- Light brown to reddish brown
- Stem very thick and club shaped
- White closely spaced small pores
- White flesh

Spore Print

Notes

Location

Site / GPS: _____ Date: _____

○ Living Tree ○ Leaf Litter ○ Mulch ○ Dead Tree or Wood ○ Grass ○ Soil ○ Other _____

Type of Tree(s) On or Near: _____

Forest Type: ○ Deciduous ○ Coniferous ○ Tropical ○ Other _____

Weather Conditions: _____

General

Size (overall height): _____ Color: _____ Spore Color: _____

Texture: ○ Tough ○ Brittle ○ Leathery ○ Woody ○ Soft ○ Slimy ○ Spongy ○ Powdery ○ Waxy ○ Rubbery ○ Watery (Other) _____

Bruising When Touched? ○ Yes ○ No   Notes: _____

Structures: ○ Cup ○ Ring ○ Warts

Cap Characteristics

Campanulate (bell-shaped)

Conical (triangular)

Cylindrical (shaped like half an egg)

Convex (outwardly rounded)

Flat (with top of uniform height)

Infundibuliform (deeply, depressed, funnel-shaped)

Depressed (with a low central region)

Umbonate (with a central bump or knob)

Surface Markings (warts, scales, slime, etc.): _____

Cap Margin: Smooth, Inrolled, Sinuous/Wavy, Other: _____

Color Changes: _____

Undercap

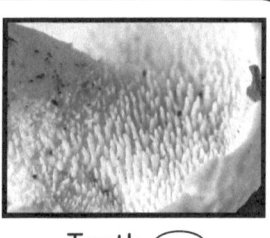

Gills ○
Attachment: Free or Decurrent
Spacing: Crowded, Close, Distant, Subdistant
Color/Bruising: _____

Pores ○
Color: _____
Pore Size: _____
Pore Pattern: _____

Teeth ○
Color: _____
Teeth Length: _____
Flesh: Soft or Tough

Gill Attachment

- ○ Free (gills not attached to stem)
- ○ Adnexed (gills attached narrowly to stem)
- ○ Sinuate (gills smoothly notched and running briefly down stem)
- ○ Adnate (gills widely attached widely to stem)
- ○ Descending (gills running down stem for some length)

Stem Shape

    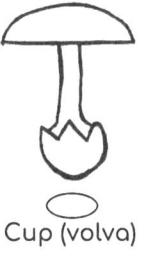

- Tapering
- Equal
- Club-Shaped
- Bulbous
- Cup (volva)

Common Mushrooms

Chanterelle
- Edible ☺
- Shape looks like bell of a trumpet
- Bright yellow/orange
- Similar look to Jack o'Lantern

Milk Mushroom
- Edible ☺
- Rounded caps that connect to an elongated, thick stem
- Smooth firm cap
- Color is pure white

Morels
- Edible ☺
- Honeycombed cap
- Most morels cap is longer than stem
- Spore print is usually light colored
- Interior is hollow

Porcini
- Edible ☺
- Large size
- Also known as king bolete
- Resembles reddish/brown hamburger bun

Shaggy Mane
- Edible ☺
- White shaggy cylindrical cap that turns black and inky with age
- Bell shape - mature
- Spore print is black

Death Cap
- Poisonous ☹
- Flattened top
- White cap with brownish scales
- Gills are free and white, turning green as they mature

False Morel
- Poisonous ☹
- Red-brown cap - irregularly lobed, like a brain
- Tube-like hollows
- Yellowish spore print
- Smooth with more wrinkles as it ages

Destroying Angel
- Poisonous ☹
- White stalk and gills
- White cap or white edge and yellowish, pinkish, or tan center
- Egg-shaped cap

Common Conecap
- Poisonous ☹
- Rust-colored brown gills and conical cap
- Surface smooth, dry
- Adnexed gills
- Slender straight stem
- Brown spore print

Deadly Galerina
- Poisonous ☹
- Brownish, sticky cap, yellowish to rusty gills, ring on stalk
- Edges are curved against gills
- Gills narrow, crowded

Lobster Mushroom
- Edible ☺
- Bumpy, reddish-orange exterior
- Fish-like taste
- Irregular shape with little to no stem
- Cracked cap

King Bolete
- Edible ☺
- Light brown to reddish brown
- Stem very thick and club shaped
- White closely spaced small pores
- White flesh

Spore Print

Notes

Location

Site / GPS: _____ Date: _____

○ Living Tree ○ Leaf Litter ○ Mulch ○ Dead Tree or Wood ○ Grass
○ Soil ○ Other _____

Type of Tree(s) On or Near: _____

Forest Type: ○ Deciduous ○ Coniferous ○ Tropical ○ Other _____

Weather Conditions: _____

General

Size (overall height): _____ Color: _____ Spore Color: _____

Texture: ○ Tough ○ Brittle ○ Leathery ○ Woody ○ Soft ○ Slimy
○ Spongy ○ Powdery ○ Waxy ○ Rubbery ○ Watery (Other) _____

Bruising When Touched? ○ Yes ○ No   Notes: _____

Structures: ○ Cup ○ Ring ○ Warts

Cap Characteristics

Campanulate (bell-shaped)

Conical (triangular)

Cylindrical (shaped like half an egg)

Convex (outwardly rounded)

Flat (with top of uniform height)

Infundibuliform (deeply, depressed, funnel-shaped)

Depressed (with a low central region)

Umbonate (with a central bump or knob)

Surface Markings (warts, scales, slime, etc.): _____

Cap Margin: Smooth, Inrolled, Sinuous/Wavy, Other: _____

Color Changes: _____

Undercap

Gills ○
Attachment: Free or Decurrent
Spacing: Crowded, Close, Distant, Subdistant
Color/Bruising: _____

Pores ○
Color: _____
Pore Size: _____
Pore Pattern: _____

Teeth ○
Color: _____
Teeth Length: _____
Flesh: Soft or Tough

Gill Attachment

- ○ **Free** (gills not attached to stem)
- ○ **Adnexed** (gills attached narrowly to stem)
- ○ **Sinuate** (gills smoothly notched and running briefly down stem)
- ○ **Adnate** (gills widely attached widely to stem)
- ○ **Descending** (gills running down stem for some length)

Stem Shape

  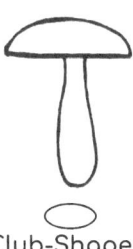  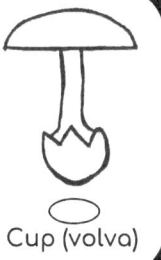

- ○ Tapering
- ○ Equal
- ○ Club-Shaped
- ○ Bulbous
- ○ Cup (volva)

Common Mushrooms

Chanterelle
- Edible ☺
- Shape looks like bell of a trumpet
- Bright yellow/orange
- Similar look to Jack o'Lantern

Shaggy Mane
- Edible ☺
- White shaggy cylindrical cap that turns black and inky with age
- Bell shape - mature
- Spore print is black

Common Conecap
- Poisonous ☹
- Rust-colored brown gills and conical cap
- Surface smooth, dry
- Adnexed gills
- Slender straight stem
- Brown spore print

Milk Mushroom
- Edible ☺
- Rounded caps that connect to an elongated, thick stem
- Smooth firm cap
- Color is pure white

Death Cap
- Poisonous ☹
- Flattened top
- White cap with brownish scales
- Gills are free and white, turning green as they mature

Deadly Galerina
- Poisonous ☹
- Brownish, sticky cap, yellowish to rusty gills, ring on stalk
- Edges are curved against gills
- Gills narrow, crowded

Morels
- Edible ☺
- Honeycombed cap
- Most morels cap is longer than stem
- Spore print is usually light colored
- Interior is hollow

False Morel
- Poisonous ☹
- Red-brown cap - irregularly lobed, like a brain
- Tube-like hollows
- Yellowish spore print
- Smooth with more wrinkles as it ages

Lobster Mushroom
- Edible ☺
- Bumpy, reddish-orange exterior
- Fish-like taste
- Irregular shape with little to no stem
- Cracked cap

Porcini
- Edible ☺
- Large size
- Also known as king bolete
- Resembles reddish/brown hamburger bun

Destroying Angel
- Poisonous ☹
- White stalk and gills
- White cap or white edge and yellowish, pinkish, or tan center
- Egg-shaped cap

King Bolete
- Edible ☺
- Light brown to reddish brown
- Stem very thick and club shaped
- White closely spaced small pores
- White flesh

Spore Print / Notes

_____
_____
_____
_____
_____
_____

Location

Site / GPS: _____ Date: _____

○ Living Tree ○ Leaf Litter ○ Mulch ○ Dead Tree or Wood ○ Grass
○ Soil ○ Other _____

Type of Tree(s) On or Near: _____

Forest Type: ○ Deciduous ○ Coniferous ○ Tropical ○ Other _____

Weather Conditions: _____

General

Size (overall height): _____ Color: _____ Spore Color: _____

Texture: ○ Tough ○ Brittle ○ Leathery ○ Woody ○ Soft ○ Slimy
○ Spongy ○ Powdery ○ Waxy ○ Rubbery ○ Watery (Other) _____

Bruising When Touched? ○ Yes ○ No   Notes: _____

Structures: ○ Cup ○ Ring ○ Warts

Cap Characteristics

Campanulate (bell-shaped)
Conical (triangular)
Cylindrical (shaped like half an egg)
Convex (outwardly rounded)

Flat (with top of uniform height)
Infundibuliform (deeply, depressed, funnel-shaped)
Depressed (with a low central region)
Umbonate (with a central bump or knob)

Surface Markings (warts, scales, slime, etc.): _____

Cap Margin: Smooth, Inrolled, Sinuous/Wavy, Other: _____

Color Changes: _____

Undercap

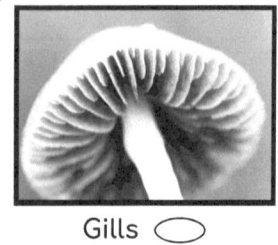
Gills ○
Attachment: Free or Decurrent
Spacing: Crowded, Close, Distant, Subdistant
Color/Bruising: _____

Pores ○
Color: _____
Pore Size: _____
Pore Pattern: _____

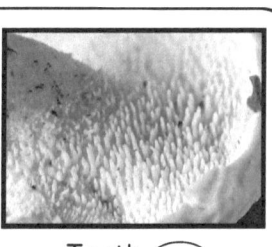
Teeth ○
Color: _____
Teeth Length: _____
Flesh: Soft or Tough

Gill Attachment

- Free (gills not attached to stem)
- Adnexed (gills attached narrowly to stem)
- Sinuate (gills smoothly notched and running briefly down stem)
- Adnate (gills widely attached widely to stem)
- Descending (gills running down stem for some length)

Stem Shape

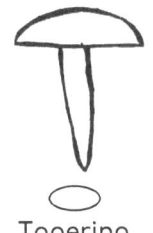    

Tapering — Equal — Club-Shaped — Bulbous — Cup (volva)

Common Mushrooms

Chanterelle
- Edible ☺
- Shape looks like bell of a trumpet
- Bright yellow/orange
- Similar look to Jack o'Lantern

Milk Mushroom
- Edible ☺
- Rounded caps that connect to an elongated, thick stem
- Smooth firm cap
- Color is pure white

Morels
- Edible ☺
- Honeycombed cap
- Most morels cap is longer than stem
- Spore print is usually light colored
- Interior is hollow

Porcini
- Edible ☺
- Large size
- Also known as king bolete
- Resembles reddish/brown hamburger bun

Shaggy Mane
- Edible ☺
- White shaggy cylindrical cap that turns black and inky with age
- Bell shape - mature
- Spore print is black

Death Cap
- Poisonous ☹
- Flattened top
- White cap with brownish scales
- Gills are free and white, turning green as they mature

False Morel
- Poisonous ☹
- Red-brown cap - irregularly lobed, like a brain
- Tube-like hollows
- Yellowish spore print
- Smooth with more wrinkles as it ages

Destroying Angel
- Poisonous ☹
- White stalk and gills
- White cap or white edge and yellowish, pinkish, or tan center
- Egg-shaped cap

Common Conecap
- Poisonous ☹
- Rust-colored brown gills and conical cap
- Surface smooth, dry
- Adnexed gills
- Slender straight stem
- Brown spore print

Deadly Galerina
- Poisonous ☹
- Brownish, sticky cap, yellowish to rusty gills, ring on stalk
- Edges are curved against gills
- Gills narrow, crowded

Lobster Mushroom
- Edible ☺
- Bumpy, reddish-orange exterior
- Fish-like taste
- Irregular shape with little to no stem
- Cracked cap

King Bolete
- Edible ☺
- Light brown to reddish brown
- Stem very thick and club shaped
- White closely spaced small pores
- White flesh

Spore Print

_____
_____
_____
_____
_____

Notes

Location

Site / GPS: _____ Date: _____

○ Living Tree ○ Leaf Litter ○ Mulch ○ Dead Tree or Wood ○ Grass
○ Soil ○ Other _____

Type of Tree(s) On or Near: _____

Forest Type: ○ Deciduous ○ Coniferous ○ Tropical ○ Other _____

Weather Conditions: _____

General

Size (overall height): _____ Color: _____ Spore Color: _____

Texture: ○ Tough ○ Brittle ○ Leathery ○ Woody ○ Soft ○ Slimy
○ Spongy ○ Powdery ○ Waxy ○ Rubbery ○ Watery (Other) _____

Bruising When Touched? ○ Yes ○ No   Notes: _____

Structures: ○ Cup ○ Ring ○ Warts

Cap Characteristics

Campanulate (bell-shaped)

Conical (triangular)

Cylindrical (shaped like half an egg)

Convex (outwardly rounded)

Flat (with top of uniform height)

Infundibuliform (deeply, depressed, funnel-shaped)

Depressed (with a low central region)

Umbonate (with a central bump or knob)

Surface Markings (warts, scales, slime, etc.): _____

Cap Margin: Smooth, Inrolled, Sinuous/Wavy, Other: _____

Color Changes: _____

Undercap

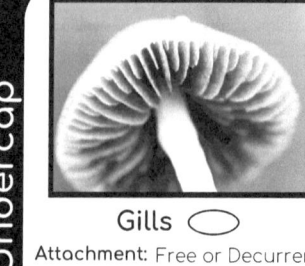

Gills ○
Attachment: Free or Decurrent
Spacing: Crowded, Close, Distant, Subdistant
Color/Bruising: _____

Pores ○
Color: _____
Pore Size: _____
Pore Pattern: _____

Teeth ○
Color: _____
Teeth Length: _____
Flesh: Soft or Tough

Gill Attachment

- **Free** (gills not attached to stem)
- **Adnexed** (gills attached narrowly to stem)
- **Sinuate** (gills smoothly notched and running briefly down stem)
- **Adnate** (gills widely attached widely to stem)
- **Descending** (gills running down stem for some length)

Stem Shape

- Tapering
- Equal
- Club-Shaped
- Bulbous
- Cup (volva)

Common Mushrooms

Chanterelle
- Edible ☺
- Shape looks like bell of a trumpet
- Bright yellow/orange
- Similar look to Jack o'Lantern

Shaggy Mane
- Edible ☺
- White shaggy cylindrical cap that turns black and inky with age
- Bell shape - mature
- Spore print is black

Common Conecap
- Poisonous ☹
- Rust-colored brown gills and conical cap
- Surface smooth, dry
- Adnexed gills
- Slender straight stem
- Brown spore print

Milk Mushroom
- Edible ☺
- Rounded caps that connect to an elongated, thick stem
- Smooth firm cap
- Color is pure white

Death Cap
- Poisonous ☹
- Flattened top
- White cap with brownish scales
- Gills are free and white, turning green as they mature

Deadly Galerina
- Poisonous ☹
- Brownish, sticky cap, yellowish to rusty gills, ring on stalk
- Edges are curved against gills
- Gills narrow, crowded

Morels
- Edible ☺
- Honeycombed cap
- Most morels cap is longer than stem
- Spore print is usually light colored
- Interior is hollow

False Morel
- Poisonous ☹
- Red-brown cap - irregularly lobed, like a brain
- Tube-like hollows
- Yellowish spore print
- Smooth with more wrinkles as it ages

Lobster Mushroom
- Edible ☺
- Bumpy, reddish-orange exterior
- Fish-like taste
- Irregular shape with little to no stem
- Cracked cap

Porcini
- Edible ☺
- Large size
- Also known as king bolete
- Resembles reddish/brown hamburger bun

Destroying Angel
- Poisonous ☹
- White stalk and gills
- White cap or white edge and yellowish, pinkish, or tan center
- Egg-shaped cap

King Bolete
- Edible ☺
- Light brown to reddish brown
- Stem very thick and club shaped
- White closely spaced small pores
- White flesh

Spore Print

Notes

_____
_____
_____
_____
_____

Location

Site / GPS: _____ Date: _____

○ Living Tree ○ Leaf Litter ○ Mulch ○ Dead Tree or Wood ○ Grass
○ Soil ○ Other _____

Type of Tree(s) On or Near: _____

Forest Type: ○ Deciduous ○ Coniferous ○ Tropical ○ Other _____

Weather Conditions: _____

General

Size (overall height): _____ Color: _____ Spore Color: _____

Texture: ○ Tough ○ Brittle ○ Leathery ○ Woody ○ Soft ○ Slimy
○ Spongy ○ Powdery ○ Waxy ○ Rubbery ○ Watery (Other) _____

Bruising When Touched? ○ Yes ○ No   Notes: _____

Structures: ○ Cup ○ Ring ○ Warts   _____

Cap Characteristics

Campanulate
(bell-shaped)

Conical
(triangular)

Cylindrical
(shaped like half an egg)

Convex
(outwardly rounded)

Flat
(with top of uniform height)

Infundibuliform
(deeply, depressed, funnel-shaped)

Depressed
(with a low central region)

Umbonate
(with a central bump or knob)

Surface Markings (warts, scales, slime, etc.): _____

Cap Margin: Smooth, Inrolled, Sinuous/Wavy, Other: _____

Color Changes: _____

Undercap

Gills ○
Attachment: Free or Decurrent
Spacing: Crowded, Close, Distant, Subdistant
Color/Bruising: _____

Pores ○
Color: _____
Pore Size: _____
Pore Pattern: _____

Teeth ○
Color: _____
Teeth Length: _____
Flesh: Soft or Tough

Gill Attachment

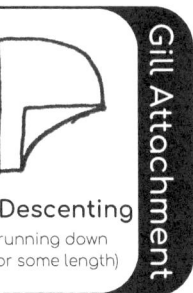

- ○ Free (gills not attached to stem)
- ○ Adnexed (gills attached narrowly to stem)
- ○ Sinuate (gills smoothly notched and running briefly down stem)
- ○ Adnate (gills widely attached widely to stem)
- ○ Descending (gills running down stem for some length)

Stem Shape

    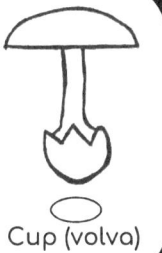

- Tapering
- Equal
- Club-Shaped
- Bulbous
- Cup (volva)

Common Mushrooms

Chanterelle
- Edible ☺
- Shape looks like bell of a trumpet
- Bright yellow/orange
- Similar look to Jack o'Lantern

Milk Mushroom
- Edible ☺
- Rounded caps that connect to an elongated, thick stem
- Smooth firm cap
- Color is pure white

Morels
- Edible ☺
- Honeycombed cap
- Most morels cap is longer than stem
- Spore print is usually light colored
- Interior is hollow

Porcini
- Edible ☺
- Large size
- Also known as king bolete
- Resembles reddish/brown hamburger bun

Shaggy Mane
- Edible ☺
- White shaggy cylindrical cap that turns black and inky with age
- Bell shape - mature
- Spore print is black

Death Cap
- Poisonous ☹
- Flattened top
- White cap with brownish scales
- Gills are free and white, turning green as they mature

False Morel
- Poisonous ☹
- Red-brown cap - irregularly lobed, like a brain
- Tube-like hollows
- Yellowish spore print
- Smooth with more wrinkles as it ages

Destroying Angel
- Poisonous ☹
- White stalk and gills
- White cap or white edge and yellowish, pinkish, or tan center
- Egg-shaped cap

Common Conecap
- Poisonous ☹
- Rust-colored brown gills and conical cap
- Surface smooth, dry
- Adnexed gills
- Slender straight stem
- Brown spore print

Deadly Galerina
- Poisonous ☹
- Brownish, sticky cap, yellowish to rusty gills, ring on stalk
- Edges are curved against gills
- Gills narrow, crowded

Lobster Mushroom
- Edible ☺
- Bumpy, reddish-orange exterior
- Fish-like taste
- Irregular shape with little to no stem
- Cracked cap

King Bolete
- Edible ☺
- Light brown to reddish brown
- Stem very thick and club shaped
- White closely spaced small pores
- White flesh

Spore Print

Notes

_____
_____
_____
_____
_____
_____

Location

Site / GPS: _____ Date: _____

○ Living Tree   ○ Leaf Litter   ○ Mulch   ○ Dead Tree or Wood   ○ Grass
○ Soil   ○ Other _____

Type of Tree(s) On or Near: _____

Forest Type: ○ Deciduous   ○ Coniferous   ○ Tropical   ○ Other _____

Weather Conditions: _____

General

Size (overall height): _____   Color: _____   Spore Color: _____

Texture: ○ Tough   ○ Brittle   ○ Leathery   ○ Woody   ○ Soft   ○ Slimy
○ Spongy   ○ Powdery   ○ Waxy   ○ Rubbery   ○ Watery   (Other) _____

Bruising When Touched? ○ Yes   ○ No   Notes: _____

Structures: ○ Cup   ○ Ring   ○ Warts

Cap Characteristics

Campanulate (bell-shaped)

Conical (triangular)

Cylindrical (shaped like half an egg)

Convex (outwardly rounded)

Flat (with top of uniform height)

Infundibuliform (deeply, depressed, funnel-shaped)

Depressed (with a low central region)

Umbonate (with a central bump or knob)

Surface Markings (warts, scales, slime, etc.): _____

Cap Margin: Smooth, Inrolled, Sinuous/Wavy, Other: _____

Color Changes: _____

Undercap

Gills ○

Attachment: Free or Decurrent
Spacing: Crowded, Close, Distant, Subdistant
Color/Bruising: _____

Pores ○

Color: _____
Pore Size: _____
Pore Pattern: _____

Teeth ○

Color: _____
Teeth Length: _____
Flesh: Soft or Tough

Gill Attachment

○ Free
(gills not attached to stem)

○ Adnexed
(gills attached narrowly to stem)

○ Sinuate
(gills smoothly notched and running briefly down stem)

○ Adnate
(gills widely attached widely to stem)

○ Descending
(gills running down stem for some length)

Stem Shape

    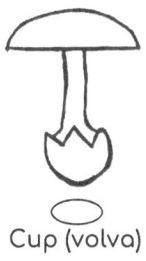

Tapering — Equal — Club-Shaped — Bulbous — Cup (volva)

Common Mushrooms

Chanterelle
- Edible ☺
- Shape looks like bell of a trumpet
- Bright yellow/orange
- Similar look to Jack o'Lantern

Milk Mushroom
- Edible ☺
- Rounded caps that connect to an elongated, thick stem
- Smooth firm cap
- Color is pure white

Morels
- Edible ☺
- Honeycombed cap
- Most morels cap is longer than stem
- Spore print is usually light colored
- Interior is hollow

Porcini
- Edible ☺
- Large size
- Also known as king bolete
- Resembles reddish/brown hamburger bun

Shaggy Mane
- Edible ☺
- White shaggy cylindrical cap that turns black and inky with age
- Bell shape - mature
- Spore print is black

Death Cap
- Poisonous ☹
- Flattened top
- White cap with brownish scales
- Gills are free and white, turning green as they mature

False Morel
- Poisonous ☹
- Red-brown cap - irregularly lobed, like a brain
- Tube-like hollows
- Yellowish spore print
- Smooth with more wrinkles as it ages

Destroying Angel
- Poisonous ☹
- White stalk and gills
- White cap or white edge and yellowish, pinkish, or tan center
- Egg-shaped cap

Common Conecap
- Poisonous ☹
- Rust-colored brown gills and conical cap
- Surface smooth, dry
- Adnexed gills
- Slender straight stem
- Brown spore print

Deadly Galerina
- Poisonous ☹
- Brownish, sticky cap, yellowish to rusty gills, ring on stalk
- Edges are curved against gills
- Gills narrow, crowded

Lobster Mushroom
- Edible ☺
- Bumpy, reddish-orange exterior
- Fish-like taste
- Irregular shape with little to no stem
- Cracked cap

King Bolete
- Edible ☺
- Light brown to reddish brown
- Stem very thick and club shaped
- White closely spaced small pores
- White flesh

Spore Print

Notes

_____
_____
_____
_____
_____

Location

Site / GPS: _____ Date: _____

○ Living Tree   ○ Leaf Litter   ○ Mulch   ○ Dead Tree or Wood   ○ Grass
○ Soil   ○ Other _____

Type of Tree(s) On or Near: _____

Forest Type: ○ Deciduous   ○ Coniferous   ○ Tropical   ○ Other _____

Weather Conditions: _____

General

Size (overall height): _____   Color: _____   Spore Color: _____

Texture: ○ Tough   ○ Brittle   ○ Leathery   ○ Woody   ○ Soft   ○ Slimy
○ Spongy   ○ Powdery   ○ Waxy   ○ Rubbery   ○ Watery   (Other) _____

Bruising When Touched? ○ Yes   ○ No   Notes: _____

Structures: ○ Cup   ○ Ring   ○ Warts   _____

Cap Characteristics

Campanulate (bell-shaped)

Conical (triangular)

Cylindrical (shaped like half an egg)

Convex (outwardly rounded)

Flat (with top of uniform height)

Infundibuliform (deeply, depressed, funnel-shaped)

Depressed (with a low central region)

Umbonate (with a central bump or knob)

Surface Markings (warts, scales, slime, etc.): _____

Cap Margin: Smooth, Inrolled, Sinuous/Wavy, Other: _____

Color Changes: _____

Undercap

Gills ○
Attachment: Free or Decurrent
Spacing: Crowded, Close, Distant, Subdistant
Color/Bruising: _____

Pores ○
Color: _____
Pore Size: _____
Pore Pattern: _____

Teeth ○
Color: _____
Teeth Length: _____
Flesh: Soft or Tough

Gill Attachment

    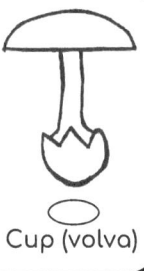

- **Free** (gills not attached to stem)
- **Adnexed** (gills attached narrowly to stem)
- **Sinuate** (gills smoothly notched and running briefly down stem)
- **Adnate** (gills widely attached widely to stem)
- **Descending** (gills running down stem for some length)

Stem Shape

- Tapering
- Equal
- Club-Shaped
- Bulbous
- Cup (volva)

Common Mushrooms

Chanterelle
- Edible ☺
- Shape looks like bell of a trumpet
- Bright yellow/orange
- Similar look to Jack o'Lantern

Shaggy Mane
- Edible ☺
- White shaggy cylindrical cap that turns black and inky with age
- Bell shape - mature
- Spore print is black

Common Conecap
- Poisonous ☹
- Rust-colored brown gills and conical cap
- Surface smooth, dry
- Adnexed gills
- Slender straight stem
- Brown spore print

Milk Mushroom
- Edible ☺
- Rounded caps that connect to an elongated, thick stem
- Smooth firm cap
- Color is pure white

Death Cap
- Poisonous ☹
- Flattened top
- White cap with brownish scales
- Gills are free and white, turning green as they mature

Deadly Galerina
- Poisonous ☹
- Brownish, sticky cap, yellowish to rusty gills, ring on stalk
- Edges are curved against gills
- Gills narrow, crowded

Morels
- Edible ☺
- Honeycombed cap
- Most morels cap is longer than stem
- Spore print is usually light colored
- Interior is hollow

False Morel
- Poisonous ☹
- Red-brown cap - irregularly lobed, like a brain
- Tube-like hollows
- Yellowish spore print
- Smooth with more wrinkles as it ages

Lobster Mushroom
- Edible ☺
- Bumpy, reddish-orange exterior
- Fish-like taste
- Irregular shape with little to no stem
- Cracked cap

Porcini
- Edible ☺
- Large size
- Also known as king bolete
- Resembles reddish/brown hamburger bun

Destroying Angel
- Poisonous ☹
- White stalk and gills
- White cap or white edge and yellowish, pinkish, or tan center
- Egg-shaped cap

King Bolete
- Edible ☺
- Light brown to reddish brown
- Stem very thick and club shaped
- White closely spaced small pores
- White flesh

Spore Print

Notes

_____
_____
_____
_____
_____
_____

Location

Site / GPS: _____ Date: _____

◯ Living Tree ◯ Leaf Litter ◯ Mulch ◯ Dead Tree or Wood ◯ Grass
◯ Soil ◯ Other _____

Type of Tree(s) On or Near: _____

Forest Type: ◯ Deciduous ◯ Coniferous ◯ Tropical ◯ Other _____

Weather Conditions: _____

General

Size (overall height): _____ Color: _____ Spore Color: _____

Texture: ◯ Tough ◯ Brittle ◯ Leathery ◯ Woody ◯ Soft ◯ Slimy
◯ Spongy ◯ Powdery ◯ Waxy ◯ Rubbery ◯ Watery (Other) _____

Bruising When Touched? ◯ Yes ◯ No   Notes: _____

Structures: ◯ Cup ◯ Ring ◯ Warts   _____

Cap Characteristics

Campanulate (bell-shaped)

Conical (triangular)

Cylindrical (shaped like half an egg)

Convex (outwardly rounded)

Flat (with top of uniform height)

Infundibuliform (deeply, depressed, funnel-shaped)

Depressed (with a low central region)

Umbonate (with a central bump or knob)

Surface Markings (warts, scales, slime, etc.): _____

Cap Margin: Smooth, Inrolled, Sinuous/Wavy, Other: _____

Color Changes: _____

Undercap

Gills ◯
Attachment: Free or Decurrent
Spacing: Crowded, Close, Distant, Subdistant
Color/Bruising: _____

Pores ◯
Color: _____
Pore Size: _____
Pore Pattern: _____

Teeth ◯
Color: _____
Teeth Length: _____
Flesh: Soft or Tough

Gill Attachment

- Free (gills not attached to stem)
- Adnexed (gills attached narrowly to stem)
- Sinuate (gills smoothly notched and running briefly down stem)
- Adnate (gills widely attached widely to stem)
- Descending (gills running down stem for some length)

Stem Shape

- Tapering
- Equal
- Club-Shaped
- Bulbous
- Cup (volva)

Common Mushrooms

Chanterelle
- Edible ☺
- Shape looks like bell of a trumpet
- Bright yellow/orange
- Similar look to Jack o'Lantern

Milk Mushroom
- Edible ☺
- Rounded caps that connect to an elongated, thick stem
- Smooth firm cap
- Color is pure white

Morels
- Edible ☺
- Honeycombed cap
- Most morels cap is longer than stem
- Spore print is usually light colored
- Interior is hollow

Porcini
- Edible ☺
- Large size
- Also known as king bolete
- Resembles reddish/brown hamburger bun

Shaggy Mane
- Edible ☺
- White shaggy cylindrical cap that turns black and inky with age
- Bell shape - mature
- Spore print is black

Death Cap
- Poisonous ☹
- Flattened top
- White cap with brownish scales
- Gills are free and white, turning green as they mature

False Morel
- Poisonous ☹
- Red-brown cap - irregularly lobed, like a brain
- Tube-like hollows
- Yellowish spore print
- Smooth with more wrinkles as it ages

Destroying Angel
- Poisonous ☹
- White stalk and gills
- White cap or white edge and yellowish, pinkish, or tan center
- Egg-shaped cap

Common Conecap
- Poisonous ☹
- Rust-colored brown gills and conical cap
- Surface smooth, dry
- Adnexed gills
- Slender straight stem
- Brown spore print

Deadly Galerina
- Poisonous ☹
- Brownish, sticky cap, yellowish to rusty gills, ring on stalk
- Edges are curved against gills
- Gills narrow, crowded

Lobster Mushroom
- Edible ☺
- Bumpy, reddish-orange exterior
- Fish-like taste
- Irregular shape with little to no stem
- Cracked cap

King Bolete
- Edible ☺
- Light brown to reddish brown
- Stem very thick and club shaped
- White closely spaced small pores
- White flesh

Spore Print

Notes

_____
_____
_____
_____
_____
_____

Location

Site / GPS: _____ Date: _____

○ Living Tree   ○ Leaf Litter   ○ Mulch   ○ Dead Tree or Wood   ○ Grass
○ Soil   ○ Other _____

Type of Tree(s) On or Near: _____

Forest Type: ○ Deciduous   ○ Coniferous   ○ Tropical   ○ Other _____

Weather Conditions: _____

General

Size (overall height): _____ Color: _____ Spore Color: _____

Texture: ○ Tough   ○ Brittle   ○ Leathery   ○ Woody   ○ Soft   ○ Slimy
○ Spongy   ○ Powdery   ○ Waxy   ○ Rubbery   ○ Watery   (Other) _____

Bruising When Touched? ○ Yes   ○ No   Notes: _____

Structures: ○ Cup   ○ Ring   ○ Warts

Cap Characteristics

Campanulate (bell-shaped)

Conical (triangular)

Cylindrical (shaped like half an egg)

Convex (outwardly rounded)

Flat (with top of uniform height)

Infundibuliform (deeply, depressed, funnel-shaped)

Depressed (with a low central region)

Umbonate (with a central bump or knob)

Surface Markings (warts, scales, slime, etc.): _____

Cap Margin: Smooth, Inrolled, Sinuous/Wavy, Other: _____

Color Changes: _____

Undercap

Gills ○
Attachment: Free or Decurrent
Spacing: Crowded, Close, Distant, Subdistant
Color/Bruising: _____

Pores ○
Color: _____
Pore Size: _____
Pore Pattern: _____

Teeth ○
Color: _____
Teeth Length: _____
Flesh: Soft or Tough

Gill Attachment

 Free
(gills not attached to stem)

 Adnexed
(gills attached narrowly to stem)

 Sinuate
(gills smoothly notched and running briefly down stem)

 Adnate
(gills widely attached widely to stem)

 Descending
(gills running down stem for some length)

Stem Shape

 Tapering

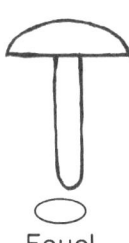 Equal

 Club-Shaped

 Bulbous

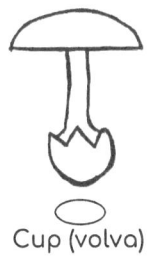 Cup (volva)

Common Mushrooms

Chanterelle
- Edible ☺
- Shape looks like bell of a trumpet
- Bright yellow/orange
- Similar look to Jack o'Lantern

Milk Mushroom
- Edible ☺
- Rounded caps that connect to an elongated, thick stem
- Smooth firm cap
- Color is pure white

Morels
- Edible ☺
- Honeycombed cap
- Most morels cap is longer than stem
- Spore print is usually light colored
- Interior is hollow

Porcini
- Edible ☺
- Large size
- Also known as king bolete
- Resembles reddish/brown hamburger bun

Shaggy Mane
- Edible ☺
- White shaggy cylindrical cap that turns black and inky with age
- Bell shape - mature
- Spore print is black

Death Cap
- Poisonous ☹
- Flattened top
- White cap with brownish scales
- Gills are free and white, turning green as they mature

False Morel
- Poisonous ☹
- Red-brown cap - irregularly lobed, like a brain
- Tube-like hollows
- Yellowish spore print
- Smooth with more wrinkles as it ages

Destroying Angel
- Poisonous ☹
- White stalk and gills
- White cap or white edge and yellowish, pinkish, or tan center
- Egg-shaped cap

Common Conecap
- Poisonous ☹
- Rust-colored brown gills and conical cap
- Surface smooth, dry
- Adnexed gills
- Slender straight stem
- Brown spore print

Deadly Galerina
- Poisonous ☹
- Brownish, sticky cap, yellowish to rusty gills, ring on stalk
- Edges are curved against gills
- Gills narrow, crowded

Lobster Mushroom
- Edible ☺
- Bumpy, reddish-orange exterior
- Fish-like taste
- Irregular shape with little to no stem
- Cracked cap

King Bolete
- Edible ☺
- Light brown to reddish brown
- Stem very thick and club shaped
- White closely spaced small pores
- White flesh

Spore Print

Notes

Location

Site / GPS: _____ Date: _____

○ Living Tree ○ Leaf Litter ○ Mulch ○ Dead Tree or Wood ○ Grass
○ Soil ○ Other _____

Type of Tree(s) On or Near: _____

Forest Type: ○ Deciduous ○ Coniferous ○ Tropical ○ Other _____

Weather Conditions: _____

General

Size (overall height): _____ Color: _____ Spore Color: _____

Texture: ○ Tough ○ Brittle ○ Leathery ○ Woody ○ Soft ○ Slimy
○ Spongy ○ Powdery ○ Waxy ○ Rubbery ○ Watery (Other) _____

Bruising When Touched? ○ Yes ○ No   Notes: _____

Structures: ○ Cup ○ Ring ○ Warts   _____

Cap Characteristics

Campanulate (bell-shaped)

Conical (triangular)

Cylindrical (shaped like half an egg)

Convex (outwardly rounded)

Flat (with top of uniform height)

Infundibuliform (deeply, depressed, funnel-shaped)

Depressed (with a low central region)

Umbonate (with a central bump or knob)

Surface Markings (warts, scales, slime, etc.): _____

Cap Margin: Smooth, Inrolled, Sinuous/Wavy, Other: _____

Color Changes: _____

Undercap

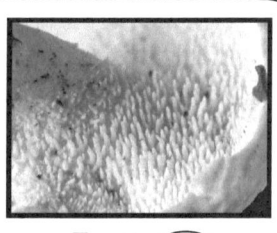

Gills ○

Attachment: Free or Decurrent

Spacing: Crowded, Close, Distant, Subdistant

Color/Bruising: _____

Pores ○

Color: _____

Pore Size: _____

Pore Pattern: _____

Teeth ○

Color: _____

Teeth Length: _____

Flesh: Soft or Tough

Gill Attachment

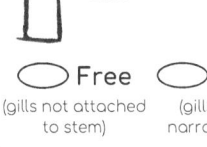

- ○ Free (gills not attached to stem)
- ○ Adnexed (gills attached narrowly to stem)
- ○ Sinuate (gills smoothly notched and running briefly down stem)
- ○ Adnate (gills widely attached widely to stem)
- ○ Descending (gills running down stem for some length)

Stem Shape

    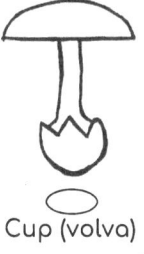

Tapering — Equal — Club-Shaped — Bulbous — Cup (volva)

Common Mushrooms

Chanterelle
- Edible ☺
- Shape looks like bell of a trumpet
- Bright yellow/orange
- Similar look to Jack o'Lantern

Milk Mushroom
- Edible ☺
- Rounded caps that connect to an elongated, thick stem
- Smooth firm cap
- Color is pure white

Morels
- Edible ☺
- Honeycombed cap
- Most morels cap is longer than stem
- Spore print is usually light colored
- Interior is hollow

Porcini
- Edible ☺
- Large size
- Also known as king bolete
- Resembles reddish/brown hamburger bun

Shaggy Mane
- Edible ☺
- White shaggy cylindrical cap that turns black and inky with age
- Bell shape - mature
- Spore print is black

Death Cap
- Poisonous ☹
- Flattened top
- White cap with brownish scales
- Gills are free and white, turning green as they mature

False Morel
- Poisonous ☹
- Red-brown cap - irregularly lobed, like a brain
- Tube-like hollows
- Yellowish spore print
- Smooth with more wrinkles as it ages

Destroying Angel
- Poisonous ☹
- White stalk and gills
- White cap or white edge and yellowish, pinkish, or tan center
- Egg-shaped cap

Common Conecap
- Poisonous ☹
- Rust-colored brown gills and conical cap
- Surface smooth, dry
- Adnexed gills
- Slender straight stem
- Brown spore print

Deadly Galerina
- Poisonous ☹
- Brownish, sticky cap, yellowish to rusty gills, ring on stalk
- Edges are curved against gills
- Gills narrow, crowded

Lobster Mushroom
- Edible ☺
- Bumpy, reddish-orange exterior
- Fish-like taste
- Irregular shape with little to no stem
- Cracked cap

King Bolete
- Edible ☺
- Light brown to reddish brown
- Stem very thick and club shaped
- White closely spaced small pores
- White flesh

Spore Print

Notes

_____
_____
_____
_____
_____

Location

Site / GPS: _____ Date: _____

○ Living Tree ○ Leaf Litter ○ Mulch ○ Dead Tree or Wood ○ Grass
○ Soil ○ Other _____

Type of Tree(s) On or Near: _____

Forest Type: ○ Deciduous ○ Coniferous ○ Tropical ○ Other _____

Weather Conditions: _____

General

Size (overall height): _____ Color: _____ Spore Color: _____

Texture: ○ Tough ○ Brittle ○ Leathery ○ Woody ○ Soft ○ Slimy
○ Spongy ○ Powdery ○ Waxy ○ Rubbery ○ Watery (Other) _____

Bruising When Touched? ○ Yes ○ No   Notes: _____

Structures: ○ Cup ○ Ring ○ Warts   _____

Cap Characteristics

Campanulate (bell-shaped)

Conical (triangular)

Cylindrical (shaped like half an egg)

Convex (outwardly rounded)

Flat (with top of uniform height)

Infundibuliform (deeply, depressed, funnel-shaped)

Depressed (with a low central region)

Umbonate (with a central bump or knob)

Surface Markings (warts, scales, slime, etc.): _____

Cap Margin: Smooth, Inrolled, Sinuous/Wavy, Other: _____

Color Changes: _____

Undercap

Gills ○
Attachment: Free or Decurrent
Spacing: Crowded, Close, Distant, Subdistant
Color/Bruising: _____

Pores ○
Color: _____
Pore Size: _____
Pore Pattern: _____

Teeth ○
Color: _____
Teeth Length: _____
Flesh: Soft or Tough

Gill Attachment

- ○ **Free** (gills not attached to stem)
- ○ **Adnexed** (gills attached narrowly to stem)
- ○ **Sinuate** (gills smoothly notched and running briefly down stem)
- ○ **Adnate** (gills widely attached widely to stem)
- ○ **Descending** (gills running down stem for some length)

Stem Shape

- **Tapering**
- **Equal**
- **Club-Shaped**
- **Bulbous**
- **Cup (volva)**

Common Mushrooms

Chanterelle
- Edible ☺
- Shape looks like bell of a trumpet
- Bright yellow/orange
- Similar look to Jack o'Lantern

Milk Mushroom
- Edible ☺
- Rounded caps that connect to an elongated, thick stem
- Smooth firm cap
- Color is pure white

Morels
- Edible ☺
- Honeycombed cap
- Most morels cap is longer than stem
- Spore print is usually light colored
- Interior is hollow

Porcini
- Edible ☺
- Large size
- Also known as king bolete
- Resembles reddish/brown hamburger bun

Shaggy Mane
- Edible ☺
- White shaggy cylindrical cap that turns black and inky with age
- Bell shape - mature
- Spore print is black

Death Cap
- Poisonous ☹
- Flattened top
- White cap with brownish scales
- Gills are free and white, turning green as they mature

False Morel
- Poisonous ☹
- Red-brown cap - irregularly lobed, like a brain
- Tube-like hollows
- Yellowish spore print
- Smooth with more wrinkles as it ages

Destroying Angel
- Poisonous ☹
- White stalk and gills
- White cap or white edge and yellowish, pinkish, or tan center
- Egg-shaped cap

Common Conecap
- Poisonous ☹
- Rust-colored brown gills and conical cap
- Surface smooth, dry
- Adnexed gills
- Slender straight stem
- Brown spore print

Deadly Galerina
- Poisonous ☹
- Brownish, sticky cap, yellowish to rusty gills, ring on stalk
- Edges are curved against gills
- Gills narrow, crowded

Lobster Mushroom
- Edible ☺
- Bumpy, reddish-orange exterior
- Fish-like taste
- Irregular shape with little to no stem
- Cracked cap

King Bolete
- Edible ☺
- Light brown to reddish brown
- Stem very thick and club shaped
- White closely spaced small pores
- White flesh

Spore Print

_____
_____
_____
_____
_____

Notes

Location

Site / GPS: _____ Date: _____

○ Living Tree ○ Leaf Litter ○ Mulch ○ Dead Tree or Wood ○ Grass
○ Soil ○ Other _____

Type of Tree(s) On or Near: _____

Forest Type: ○ Deciduous ○ Coniferous ○ Tropical ○ Other _____

Weather Conditions: _____

General

Size (overall height): _____ Color: _____ Spore Color: _____

Texture: ○ Tough ○ Brittle ○ Leathery ○ Woody ○ Soft ○ Slimy
○ Spongy ○ Powdery ○ Waxy ○ Rubbery ○ Watery (Other) _____

Bruising When Touched? ○ Yes ○ No Notes: _____

Structures: ○ Cup ○ Ring ○ Warts

Cap Characteristics

Campanulate (bell-shaped)

Conical (triangular)

Cylindrical (shaped like half an egg)

Convex (outwardly rounded)

Flat (with top of uniform height)

Infundibuliform (deeply, depressed, funnel-shaped)

Depressed (with a low central region)

Umbonate (with a central bump or knob)

Surface Markings (warts, scales, slime, etc.): _____

Cap Margin: Smooth, Inrolled, Sinuous/Wavy, Other: _____

Color Changes: _____

Undercap

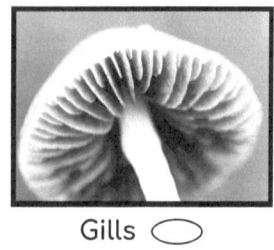

Gills ○
Attachment: Free or Decurrent
Spacing: Crowded, Close, Distant, Subdistant
Color/Bruising: _____

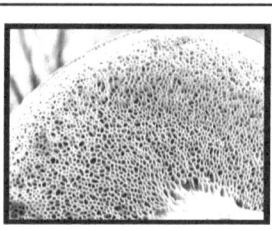

Pores ○
Color: _____
Pore Size: _____
Pore Pattern: _____

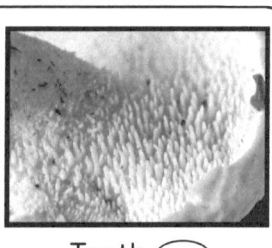

Teeth ○
Color: _____
Teeth Length: _____
Flesh: Soft or Tough

Gill Attachment

- **Free** (gills not attached to stem)
- **Adnexed** (gills attached narrowly to stem)
- **Sinuate** (gills smoothly notched and running briefly down stem)
- **Adnate** (gills widely attached widely to stem)
- **Descending** (gills running down stem for some length)

Stem Shape

    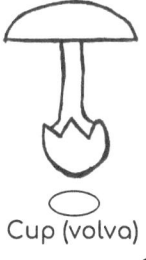

- **Tapering**
- **Equal**
- **Club-Shaped**
- **Bulbous**
- **Cup (volva)**

Common Mushrooms

Chanterelle
- Edible ☺
- Shape looks like bell of a trumpet
- Bright yellow/orange
- Similar look to Jack o'Lantern

Milk Mushroom
- Edible ☺
- Rounded caps that connect to an elongated, thick stem
- Smooth firm cap
- Color is pure white

Morels
- Edible ☺
- Honeycombed cap
- Most morels cap is longer than stem
- Spore print is usually light colored
- Interior is hollow

Porcini
- Edible ☺
- Large size
- Also known as king bolete
- Resembles reddish/brown hamburger bun

Shaggy Mane
- Edible ☺
- White shaggy cylindrical cap that turns black and inky with age
- Bell shape - mature
- Spore print is black

Death Cap
- Poisonous ☹
- Flattened top
- White cap with brownish scales
- Gills are free and white, turning green as they mature

False Morel
- Poisonous ☹
- Red-brown cap - irregularly lobed, like a brain
- Tube-like hollows
- Yellowish spore print
- Smooth with more wrinkles as it ages

Destroying Angel
- Poisonous ☹
- White stalk and gills
- White cap or white edge and yellowish, pinkish, or tan center
- Egg-shaped cap

Common Conecap
- Poisonous ☹
- Rust-colored brown gills and conical cap
- Surface smooth, dry
- Adnexed gills
- Slender straight stem
- Brown spore print

Deadly Galerina
- Poisonous ☹
- Brownish, sticky cap, yellowish to rusty gills, ring on stalk
- Edges are curved against gills
- Gills narrow, crowded

Lobster Mushroom
- Edible ☺
- Bumpy, reddish-orange exterior
- Fish-like taste
- Irregular shape with little to no stem
- Cracked cap

King Bolete
- Edible ☺
- Light brown to reddish brown
- Stem very thick and club shaped
- White closely spaced small pores
- White flesh

Spore Print

Notes

Location

Site / GPS: _____ Date: _____

◯ Living Tree ◯ Leaf Litter ◯ Mulch ◯ Dead Tree or Wood ◯ Grass
◯ Soil ◯ Other _____

Type of Tree(s) On or Near: _____

Forest Type: ◯ Deciduous ◯ Coniferous ◯ Tropical ◯ Other _____

Weather Conditions: _____

General

Size (overall height): _____   Color: _____   Spore Color: _____

Texture: ◯ Tough ◯ Brittle ◯ Leathery ◯ Woody ◯ Soft ◯ Slimy
◯ Spongy ◯ Powdery ◯ Waxy ◯ Rubbery ◯ Watery (Other) _____

Bruising When Touched? ◯ Yes ◯ No   Notes: _____

Structures: ◯ Cup ◯ Ring ◯ Warts   _____

Cap Characteristics

Campanulate (bell-shaped)

Conical (triangular)

Cylindrical (shaped like half an egg)

Convex (outwardly rounded)

Flat (with top of uniform height)

Infundibuliform (deeply, depressed, funnel-shaped)

Depressed (with a low central region)

Umbonate (with a central bump or knob)

Surface Markings (warts, scales, slime, etc.): _____

Cap Margin: Smooth, Inrolled, Sinuous/Wavy, Other: _____

Color Changes: _____

Undercap

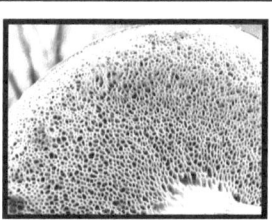

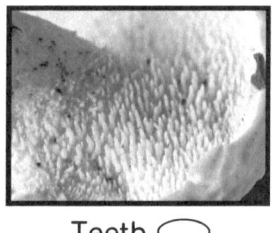

Gills ◯
Attachment: Free or Decurrent
Spacing: Crowded, Close, Distant, Subdistant
Color/Bruising: _____

Pores ◯
Color: _____
Pore Size: _____
Pore Pattern: _____

Teeth ◯
Color: _____
Teeth Length: _____
Flesh: Soft or Tough

Gill Attachment

- **Free** (gills not attached to stem)
- **Adnexed** (gills attached narrowly to stem)
- **Sinuate** (gills smoothly notched and running briefly down stem)
- **Adnate** (gills widely attached widely to stem)
- **Descending** (gills running down stem for some length)

Stem Shape

- Tapering
- Equal
- Club-Shaped
- Bulbous
- Cup (volva)

Common Mushrooms

Chanterelle
- Edible ☺
- Shape looks like bell of a trumpet
- Bright yellow/orange
- Similar look to Jack o'Lantern

Milk Mushroom
- Edible ☺
- Rounded caps that connect to an elongated, thick stem
- Smooth firm cap
- Color is pure white

Morels
- Edible ☺
- Honeycombed cap
- Most morels cap is longer than stem
- Spore print is usually light colored
- Interior is hollow

Porcini
- Edible ☺
- Large size
- Also known as king bolete
- Resembles reddish/brown hamburger bun

Shaggy Mane
- Edible ☺
- White shaggy cylindrical cap that turns black and inky with age
- Bell shape - mature
- Spore print is black

Death Cap
- Poisonous ☹
- Flattened top
- White cap with brownish scales
- Gills are free and white, turning green as they mature

False Morel
- Poisonous ☹
- Red-brown cap - irregularly lobed, like a brain
- Tube-like hollows
- Yellowish spore print
- Smooth with more wrinkles as it ages

Destroying Angel
- Poisonous ☹
- White stalk and gills
- White cap or white edge and yellowish, pinkish, or tan center
- Egg-shaped cap

Common Conecap
- Poisonous ☹
- Rust-colored brown gills and conical cap
- Surface smooth, dry
- Adnexed gills
- Slender straight stem
- Brown spore print

Deadly Galerina
- Poisonous ☹
- Brownish, sticky cap, yellowish to rusty gills, ring on stalk
- Edges are curved against gills
- Gills narrow, crowded

Lobster Mushroom
- Edible ☺
- Bumpy, reddish-orange exterior
- Fish-like taste
- Irregular shape with little to no stem
- Cracked cap

King Bolete
- Edible ☺
- Light brown to reddish brown
- Stem very thick and club shaped
- White closely spaced small pores
- White flesh

Spore Print

Notes

_____
_____
_____
_____
_____
_____

Location

Site / GPS: _____ Date: _____

○ Living Tree ○ Leaf Litter ○ Mulch ○ Dead Tree or Wood ○ Grass
○ Soil ○ Other _____

Type of Tree(s) On or Near: _____

Forest Type: ○ Deciduous ○ Coniferous ○ Tropical ○ Other _____

Weather Conditions: _____

General

Size (overall height): _____ Color: _____ Spore Color: _____

Texture: ○ Tough ○ Brittle ○ Leathery ○ Woody ○ Soft ○ Slimy
○ Spongy ○ Powdery ○ Waxy ○ Rubbery ○ Watery (Other) _____

Bruising When Touched? ○ Yes ○ No   Notes: _____

Structures: ○ Cup ○ Ring ○ Warts

Cap Characteristics

Campanulate (bell-shaped)

Conical (triangular)

Cylindrical (shaped like half an egg)

Convex (outwardly rounded)

Flat (with top of uniform height)

Infundibuliform (deeply, depressed, funnel-shaped)

Depressed (with a low central region)

Umbonate (with a central bump or knob)

Surface Markings (warts, scales, slime, etc.): _____

Cap Margin: Smooth, Inrolled, Sinuous/Wavy, Other: _____

Color Changes: _____

Undercap

Gills ○
Attachment: Free or Decurrent
Spacing: Crowded, Close, Distant, Subdistant
Color/Bruising: _____

Pores ○
Color: _____
Pore Size: _____
Pore Pattern: _____

Teeth ○
Color: _____
Teeth Length: _____
Flesh: Soft or Tough

Gill Attachment

○ Free (gills not attached to stem)
○ Adnexed (gills attached narrowly to stem)
○ Sinuate (gills smoothly notched and running briefly down stem)
○ Adnate (gills widely attached widely to stem)
○ Descending (gills running down stem for some length)

  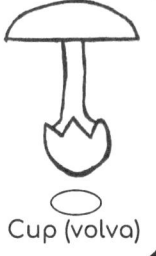

Stem Shape

Tapering | Equal | Club-Shaped | Bulbous | Cup (volva)

Common Mushrooms

Chanterelle
- Edible ☺
- Shape looks like bell of a trumpet
- Bright yellow/orange
- Similar look to Jack o'Lantern

Milk Mushroom
- Edible ☺
- Rounded caps that connect to an elongated, thick stem
- Smooth firm cap
- Color is pure white

Morels
- Edible ☺
- Honeycombed cap
- Most morels cap is longer than stem
- Spore print is usually light colored
- Interior is hollow

Porcini
- Edible ☺
- Large size
- Also known as king bolete
- Resembles reddish/brown hamburger bun

Shaggy Mane
- Edible ☺
- White shaggy cylindrical cap that turns black and inky with age
- Bell shape - mature
- Spore print is black

Death Cap
- Poisonous ☹
- Flattened top
- White cap with brownish scales
- Gills are free and white, turning green as they mature

False Morel
- Poisonous ☹
- Red-brown cap - irregularly lobed, like a brain
- Tube-like hollows
- Yellowish spore print
- Smooth with more wrinkles as it ages

Destroying Angel
- Poisonous ☹
- White stalk and gills
- White cap or white edge and yellowish, pinkish, or tan center
- Egg-shaped cap

Common Conecap
- Poisonous ☹
- Rust-colored brown gills and conical cap
- Surface smooth, dry
- Adnexed gills
- Slender straight stem
- Brown spore print

Deadly Galerina
- Poisonous ☹
- Brownish, sticky cap, yellowish to rusty gills, ring on stalk
- Edges are curved against gills
- Gills narrow, crowded

Lobster Mushroom
- Edible ☺
- Bumpy, reddish-orange exterior
- Fish-like taste
- Irregular shape with little to no stem
- Cracked cap

King Bolete
- Edible ☺
- Light brown to reddish brown
- Stem very thick and club shaped
- White closely spaced small pores
- White flesh

Spore Print

Notes

_____
_____
_____
_____
_____
_____

Location

Site / GPS: _____ Date: _____

○ Living Tree   ○ Leaf Litter   ○ Mulch   ○ Dead Tree or Wood   ○ Grass
○ Soil   ○ Other _____

Type of Tree(s) On or Near: _____

Forest Type: ○ Deciduous   ○ Coniferous   ○ Tropical   ○ Other _____

Weather Conditions: _____

General

Size (overall height): _____   Color: _____   Spore Color: _____

Texture: ○ Tough ○ Brittle ○ Leathery ○ Woody ○ Soft ○ Slimy
○ Spongy ○ Powdery ○ Waxy ○ Rubbery ○ Watery (Other) _____

Bruising When Touched? ○ Yes ○ No   Notes: _____

Structures: ○ Cup ○ Ring ○ Warts

Cap Characteristics

Campanulate (bell-shaped)

Conical (triangular)

Cylindrical (shaped like half an egg)

Convex (outwardly rounded)

Flat (with top of uniform height)

Infundibuliform (deeply, depressed, funnel-shaped)

Depressed (with a low central region)

Umbonate (with a central bump or knob)

Surface Markings (warts, scales, slime, etc.): _____

Cap Margin: Smooth, Inrolled, Sinuous/Wavy, Other: _____

Color Changes: _____

Undercap

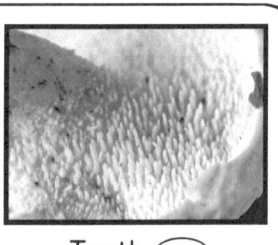

Gills ○

Attachment: Free or Decurrent

Spacing: Crowded, Close, Distant, Subdistant

Color/Bruising: _____

Pores ○

Color: _____

Pore Size: _____

Pore Pattern: _____

Teeth ○

Color: _____

Teeth Length: _____

Flesh: Soft or Tough

Gill Attachment

- Free (gills not attached to stem)
- Adnexed (gills attached narrowly to stem)
- Sinuate (gills smoothly notched and running briefly down stem)
- Adnate (gills widely attached widely to stem)
- Descenting (gills running down stem for some length)

Stem Shape

- Tapering
- Equal
- Club-Shaped
- Bulbous
- Cup (volva)

Common Mushrooms

Chanterelle
- Edible ☺
- Shape looks like bell of a trumpet
- Bright yellow/orange
- Similar look to Jack o'Lantern

Shaggy Mane
- Edible ☺
- White shaggy cylindrical cap that turns black and inky with age
- Bell shape - mature
- Spore print is black

Common Conecap
- Poisonous ☹
- Rust-colored brown gills and conical cap
- Surface smooth, dry
- Adnexed gills
- Slender straight stem
- Brown spore print

Milk Mushroom
- Edible ☺
- Rounded caps that connect to an elongated, thick stem
- Smooth firm cap
- Color is pure white

Death Cap
- Poisonous ☹
- Flattened top
- White cap with brownish scales
- Gills are free and white, turning green as they mature

Deadly Galerina
- Poisonous ☹
- Brownish, sticky cap, yellowish to rusty gills, ring on stalk
- Edges are curved against gills
- Gills narrow, crowded

Morels
- Edible ☺
- Honeycombed cap
- Most morels cap is longer than stem
- Spore print is usually light colored
- Interior is hollow

False Morel
- Poisonous ☹
- Red-brown cap - irregularly lobed, like a brain
- Tube-like hollows
- Yellowish spore print
- Smooth with more wrinkles as it ages

Lobster Mushroom
- Edible ☺
- Bumpy, reddish-orange exterior
- Fish-like taste
- Irregular shape with little to no stem
- Cracked cap

Porcini
- Edible ☺
- Large size
- Also known as king bolete
- Resembles reddish/brown hamburger bun

Destroying Angel
- Poisonous ☹
- White stalk and gills
- White cap or white edge and yellowish, pinkish, or tan center
- Egg-shaped cap

King Bolete
- Edible ☺
- Light brown to reddish brown
- Stem very thick and club shaped
- White closely spaced small pores
- White flesh

Spore Print

Notes

___
___
___
___
___

Location

Site / GPS: _____ Date: _____

○ Living Tree ○ Leaf Litter ○ Mulch ○ Dead Tree or Wood ○ Grass
○ Soil ○ Other _____

Type of Tree(s) On or Near: _____

Forest Type: ○ Deciduous ○ Coniferous ○ Tropical ○ Other _____

Weather Conditions: _____

General

Size (overall height): _____ Color: _____ Spore Color: _____

Texture: ○ Tough ○ Brittle ○ Leathery ○ Woody ○ Soft ○ Slimy
○ Spongy ○ Powdery ○ Waxy ○ Rubbery ○ Watery (Other) _____

Bruising When Touched? ○ Yes ○ No   Notes: _____

Structures: ○ Cup ○ Ring ○ Warts   _____

Cap Characteristics

Campanulate (bell-shaped)
Conical (triangular)
Cylindrical (shaped like half an egg)
Convex (outwardly rounded)

Flat (with top of uniform height)
Infundibuliform (deeply, depressed, funnel-shaped)
Depressed (with a low central region)
Umbonate (with a central bump or knob)

Surface Markings (warts, scales, slime, etc.): _____

Cap Margin: Smooth, Inrolled, Sinuous/Wavy, Other: _____

Color Changes: _____

Undercap

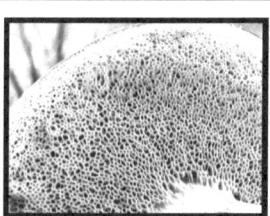
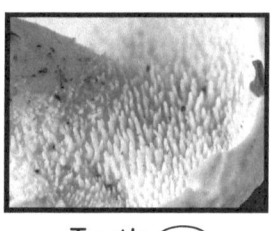

Gills ○
Attachment: Free or Decurrent
Spacing: Crowded, Close, Distant, Subdistant
Color/Bruising: _____

Pores ○
Color: _____
Pore Size: _____
Pore Pattern: _____

Teeth ○
Color: _____
Teeth Length: _____
Flesh: Soft or Tough

Gill Attachment

- Free (gills not attached to stem)
- Adnexed (gills attached narrowly to stem)
- Sinuate (gills smoothly notched and running briefly down stem)
- Adnate (gills widely attached widely to stem)
- Descending (gills running down stem for some length)

Stem Shape

- Tapering
- Equal
- Club-Shaped
- Bulbous
- Cup (volva)

Common Mushrooms

Chanterelle
- Edible ☺
- Shape looks like bell of a trumpet
- Bright yellow/orange
- Similar look to Jack o'Lantern

Milk Mushroom
- Edible ☺
- Rounded caps that connect to an elongated, thick stem
- Smooth firm cap
- Color is pure white

Morels
- Edible ☺
- Honeycombed cap
- Most morels cap is longer than stem
- Spore print is usually light colored
- Interior is hollow

Porcini
- Edible ☺
- Large size
- Also known as king bolete
- Resembles reddish/brown hamburger bun

Shaggy Mane
- Edible ☺
- White shaggy cylindrical cap that turns black and inky with age
- Bell shape - mature
- Spore print is black

Death Cap
- Poisonous ☹
- Flattened top
- White cap with brownish scales
- Gills are free and white, turning green as they mature

False Morel
- Poisonous ☹
- Red-brown cap - irregularly lobed, like a brain
- Tube-like hollows
- Yellowish spore print
- Smooth with more wrinkles as it ages

Destroying Angel
- Poisonous ☹
- White stalk and gills
- White cap or white edge and yellowish, pinkish, or tan center
- Egg-shaped cap

Common Conecap
- Poisonous ☹
- Rust-colored brown gills and conical cap
- Surface smooth, dry
- Adnexed gills
- Slender straight stem
- Brown spore print

Deadly Galerina
- Poisonous ☹
- Brownish, sticky cap, yellowish to rusty gills, ring on stalk
- Edges are curved against gills
- Gills narrow, crowded

Lobster Mushroom
- Edible ☺
- Bumpy, reddish-orange exterior
- Fish-like taste
- Irregular shape with little to no stem
- Cracked cap

King Bolete
- Edible ☺
- Light brown to reddish brown
- Stem very thick and club shaped
- White closely spaced small pores
- White flesh

Spore Print

Notes

Location

Site / GPS: _____ Date: _____

◯ Living Tree ◯ Leaf Litter ◯ Mulch ◯ Dead Tree or Wood ◯ Grass
◯ Soil ◯ Other _____

Type of Tree(s) On or Near: _____

Forest Type: ◯ Deciduous ◯ Coniferous ◯ Tropical ◯ Other _____

Weather Conditions: _____

General

Size (overall height): _____ Color: _____ Spore Color: _____

Texture: ◯ Tough ◯ Brittle ◯ Leathery ◯ Woody ◯ Soft ◯ Slimy
◯ Spongy ◯ Powdery ◯ Waxy ◯ Rubbery ◯ Watery (Other) _____

Bruising When Touched? ◯ Yes ◯ No Notes: _____

Structures: ◯ Cup ◯ Ring ◯ Warts _____

Cap Characteristics

Campanulate (bell-shaped)

Conical (triangular)

Cylindrical (shaped like half an egg)

Convex (outwardly rounded)

Flat (with top of uniform height)

Infundibuliform (deeply, depressed, funnel-shaped)

Depressed (with a low central region)

Umbonate (with a central bump or knob)

Surface Markings (warts, scales, slime, etc.): _____

Cap Margin: Smooth, Inrolled, Sinuous/Wavy, Other: _____

Color Changes: _____

Undercap

Gills ◯
Attachment: Free or Decurrent
Spacing: Crowded, Close, Distant, Subdistant
Color/Bruising: _____

Pores ◯
Color: _____
Pore Size: _____
Pore Pattern: _____

Teeth ◯
Color: _____
Teeth Length: _____
Flesh: Soft or Tough

Gill Attachment

- ○ Free (gills not attached to stem)
- ○ Adnexed (gills attached narrowly to stem)
- ○ Sinuate (gills smoothly notched and running briefly down stem)
- ○ Adnate (gills widely attached widely to stem)
- ○ Descending (gills running down stem for some length)

Stem Shape

- ○ Tapering
- ○ Equal
- ○ Club-Shaped
- ○ Bulbous
- ○ Cup (volva)

Common Mushrooms

Chanterelle
- Edible ☺
- Shape looks like bell of a trumpet
- Bright yellow/orange
- Similar look to Jack o'Lantern

Milk Mushroom
- Edible ☺
- Rounded caps that connect to an elongated, thick stem
- Smooth firm cap
- Color is pure white

Morels
- Edible ☺
- Honeycombed cap
- Most morels cap is longer than stem
- Spore print is usually light colored
- Interior is hollow

Porcini
- Edible ☺
- Large size
- Also known as king bolete
- Resembles reddish/brown hamburger bun

Shaggy Mane
- Edible ☺
- White shaggy cylindrical cap that turns black and inky with age
- Bell shape - mature
- Spore print is black

Death Cap
- Poisonous ☹
- Flattened top
- White cap with brownish scales
- Gills are free and white, turning green as they mature

False Morel
- Poisonous ☹
- Red-brown cap - irregularly lobed, like a brain
- Tube-like hollows
- Yellowish spore print
- Smooth with more wrinkles as it ages

Destroying Angel
- Poisonous ☹
- White stalk and gills
- White cap or white edge and yellowish, pinkish, or tan center
- Egg-shaped cap

Common Conecap
- Poisonous ☹
- Rust-colored brown gills and conical cap
- Surface smooth, dry
- Adnexed gills
- Slender straight stem
- Brown spore print

Deadly Galerina
- Poisonous ☹
- Brownish, sticky cap, yellowish to rusty gills, ring on stalk
- Edges are curved against gills
- Gills narrow, crowded

Lobster Mushroom
- Edible ☺
- Bumpy, reddish-orange exterior
- Fish-like taste
- Irregular shape with little to no stem
- Cracked cap

King Bolete
- Edible ☺
- Light brown to reddish brown
- Stem very thick and club shaped
- White closely spaced small pores
- White flesh

Spore Print

_____
_____
_____
_____
_____
_____

Notes

Location

Site / GPS: _____ Date: _____

◯ Living Tree ◯ Leaf Litter ◯ Mulch ◯ Dead Tree or Wood ◯ Grass
◯ Soil ◯ Other _____

Type of Tree(s) On or Near: _____

Forest Type: ◯ Deciduous ◯ Coniferous ◯ Tropical ◯ Other _____

Weather Conditions: _____

General

Size (overall height): _____ Color: _____ Spore Color: _____

Texture: ◯ Tough ◯ Brittle ◯ Leathery ◯ Woody ◯ Soft ◯ Slimy
◯ Spongy ◯ Powdery ◯ Waxy ◯ Rubbery ◯ Watery (Other) _____

Bruising When Touched? ◯ Yes ◯ No   Notes: _____

Structures: ◯ Cup ◯ Ring ◯ Warts   _____

Cap Characteristics

Campanulate (bell-shaped)

Conical (triangular)

Cylindrical (shaped like half an egg)

Convex (outwardly rounded)

Flat (with top of uniform height)

Infundibuliform (deeply, depressed, funnel-shaped)

Depressed (with a low central region)

Umbonate (with a central bump or knob)

Surface Markings (warts, scales, slime, etc.): _____

Cap Margin: Smooth, Inrolled, Sinuous/Wavy, Other: _____

Color Changes: _____

Undercap

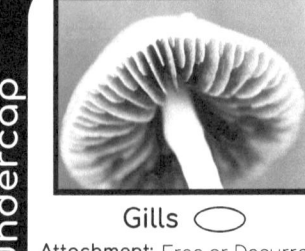

Gills ◯
Attachment: Free or Decurrent
Spacing: Crowded, Close, Distant, Subdistant
Color/Bruising: _____

Pores ◯
Color: _____
Pore Size: _____
Pore Pattern: _____

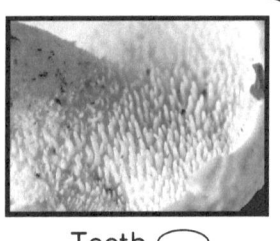

Teeth ◯
Color: _____
Teeth Length: _____
Flesh: Soft or Tough

Gill Attachment

- Free (gills not attached to stem)
- Adnexed (gills attached narrowly to stem)
- Sinuate (gills smoothly notched and running briefly down stem)
- Adnate (gills widely attached widely to stem)
- Descending (gills running down stem for some length)

Stem Shape

    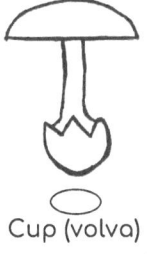

Tapering | Equal | Club-Shaped | Bulbous | Cup (volva)

Common Mushrooms

Chanterelle
- Edible ☺
- Shape looks like bell of a trumpet
- Bright yellow/orange
- Similar look to Jack o'Lantern

Milk Mushroom
- Edible ☺
- Rounded caps that connect to an elongated, thick stem
- Smooth firm cap
- Color is pure white

Morels
- Edible ☺
- Honeycombed cap
- Most morels cap is longer than stem
- Spore print is usually light colored
- Interior is hollow

Porcini
- Edible ☺
- Large size
- Also known as king bolete
- Resembles reddish/brown hamburger bun

Shaggy Mane
- Edible ☺
- White shaggy cylindrical cap that turns black and inky with age
- Bell shape - mature
- Spore print is black

Death Cap
- Poisonous ☹
- Flattened top
- White cap with brownish scales
- Gills are free and white, turning green as they mature

False Morel
- Poisonous ☹
- Red-brown cap - irregularly lobed, like a brain
- Tube-like hollows
- Yellowish spore print
- Smooth with more wrinkles as it ages

Destroying Angel
- Poisonous ☹
- White stalk and gills
- White cap or white edge and yellowish, pinkish, or tan center
- Egg-shaped cap

Common Conecap
- Poisonous ☹
- Rust-colored brown gills and conical cap
- Surface smooth, dry
- Adnexed gills
- Slender straight stem
- Brown spore print

Deadly Galerina
- Poisonous ☹
- Brownish, sticky cap, yellowish to rusty gills, ring on stalk
- Edges are curved against gills
- Gills narrow, crowded

Lobster Mushroom
- Edible ☺
- Bumpy, reddish-orange exterior
- Fish-like taste
- Irregular shape with little to no stem
- Cracked cap

King Bolete
- Edible ☺
- Light brown to reddish brown
- Stem very thick and club shaped
- White closely spaced small pores
- White flesh

Spore Print

Notes

___
___
___
___
___

Location

Site / GPS: _____ Date: _____

○ Living Tree ○ Leaf Litter ○ Mulch ○ Dead Tree or Wood ○ Grass
○ Soil ○ Other _____

Type of Tree(s) On or Near: _____

Forest Type: ○ Deciduous ○ Coniferous ○ Tropical ○ Other _____

Weather Conditions: _____

General

Size (overall height): _____ Color: _____ Spore Color: _____

Texture: ○ Tough ○ Brittle ○ Leathery ○ Woody ○ Soft ○ Slimy
○ Spongy ○ Powdery ○ Waxy ○ Rubbery ○ Watery (Other) _____

Bruising When Touched? ○ Yes ○ No Notes: _____

Structures: ○ Cup ○ Ring ○ Warts _____

Cap Characteristics

Campanulate (bell-shaped)

Conical (triangular)

Cylindrical (shaped like half an egg)

Convex (outwardly rounded)

Flat (with top of uniform height)

Infundibuliform (deeply, depressed, funnel-shaped)

Depressed (with a low central region)

Umbonate (with a central bump or knob)

Surface Markings (warts, scales, slime, etc.): _____

Cap Margin: Smooth, Inrolled, Sinuous/Wavy, Other: _____

Color Changes: _____

Undercap

Gills ○
Attachment: Free or Decurrent
Spacing: Crowded, Close, Distant, Subdistant
Color/Bruising: _____

Pores ○
Color: _____
Pore Size: _____
Pore Pattern: _____

Teeth ○
Color: _____
Teeth Length: _____
Flesh: Soft or Tough

Gill Attachment

 ○ Free
(gills not attached to stem)

 ○ Adnexed
(gills attached narrowly to stem)

 ○ Sinuate
(gills smoothly notched and running briefly down stem)

 ○ Adnate
(gills widely attached widely to stem)

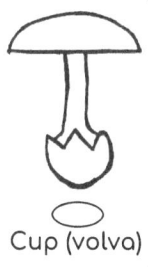 ○ Descending
(gills running down stem for some length)

Stem Shape

Tapering | Equal | Club-Shaped | Bulbous | Cup (volva)

Common Mushrooms

Chanterelle
- Edible ☺
- Shape looks like bell of a trumpet
- Bright yellow/orange
- Similar look to Jack o'Lantern

Shaggy Mane
- Edible ☺
- White shaggy cylindrical cap that turns black and inky with age
- Bell shape - mature
- Spore print is black

Common Conecap
- Poisonous ☹
- Rust-colored brown gills and conical cap
- Surface smooth, dry
- Adnexed gills
- Slender straight stem
- Brown spore print

Milk Mushroom
- Edible ☺
- Rounded caps that connect to an elongated, thick stem
- Smooth firm cap
- Color is pure white

Death Cap
- Poisonous ☹
- Flattened top
- White cap with brownish scales
- Gills are free and white, turning green as they mature

Deadly Galerina
- Poisonous ☹
- Brownish, sticky cap, yellowish to rusty gills, ring on stalk
- Edges are curved against gills
- Gills narrow, crowded

Morels
- Edible ☺
- Honeycombed cap
- Most morels cap is longer than stem
- Spore print is usually light colored
- Interior is hollow

False Morel
- Poisonous ☹
- Red-brown cap - irregularly lobed, like a brain
- Tube-like hollows
- Yellowish spore print
- Smooth with more wrinkles as it ages

Lobster Mushroom
- Edible ☺
- Bumpy, reddish-orange exterior
- Fish-like taste
- Irregular shape with little to no stem
- Cracked cap

Porcini
- Edible ☺
- Large size
- Also known as king bolete
- Resembles reddish/brown hamburger bun

Destroying Angel
- Poisonous ☹
- White stalk and gills
- White cap or white edge and yellowish, pinkish, or tan center
- Egg-shaped cap

King Bolete
- Edible ☺
- Light brown to reddish brown
- Stem very thick and club shaped
- White closely spaced small pores
- White flesh

Spore Print

Notes

Location

Site / GPS: _____ Date: _____

○ Living Tree ○ Leaf Litter ○ Mulch ○ Dead Tree or Wood ○ Grass
○ Soil ○ Other _____

Type of Tree(s) On or Near: _____

Forest Type: ○ Deciduous ○ Coniferous ○ Tropical ○ Other _____

Weather Conditions: _____

General

Size (overall height): _____ Color: _____ Spore Color: _____

Texture: ○ Tough ○ Brittle ○ Leathery ○ Woody ○ Soft ○ Slimy
○ Spongy ○ Powdery ○ Waxy ○ Rubbery ○ Watery (Other) _____

Bruising When Touched? ○ Yes ○ No Notes: _____

Structures: ○ Cup ○ Ring ○ Warts _____

Cap Characteristics

Campanulate (bell-shaped)

Conical (triangular)

Cylindrical (shaped like half an egg)

Convex (outwardly rounded)

Flat (with top of uniform height)

Infundibuliform (deeply, depressed, funnel-shaped)

Depressed (with a low central region)

Umbonate (with a central bump or knob)

Surface Markings (warts, scales, slime, etc.): _____

Cap Margin: Smooth, Inrolled, Sinuous/Wavy, Other: _____

Color Changes: _____

Undercap

Gills ○
Attachment: Free or Decurrent
Spacing: Crowded, Close, Distant, Subdistant
Color/Bruising: _____

Pores ○
Color: _____
Pore Size: _____
Pore Pattern: _____

Teeth ○
Color: _____
Teeth Length: _____
Flesh: Soft or Tough

Gill Attachment

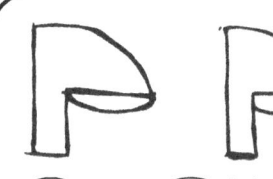

- ○ Free (gills not attached to stem)
- ○ Adnexed (gills attached narrowly to stem)
- ○ Sinuate (gills smoothly notched and running briefly down stem)
- ○ Adnate (gills widely attached widely to stem)
- ○ Descending (gills running down stem for some length)

Stem Shape

   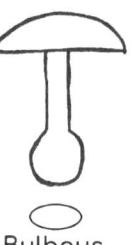 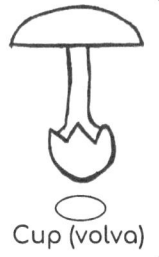

Tapering   Equal   Club-Shaped   Bulbous   Cup (volva)

Common Mushrooms

Chanterelle
- Edible ☺
- Shape looks like bell of a trumpet
- Bright yellow/orange
- Similar look to Jack o'Lantern

Milk Mushroom
- Edible ☺
- Rounded caps that connect to an elongated, thick stem
- Smooth firm cap
- Color is pure white

Morels
- Edible ☺
- Honeycombed cap
- Most morels cap is longer than stem
- Spore print is usually light colored
- Interior is hollow

Porcini
- Edible ☺
- Large size
- Also known as king bolete
- Resembles reddish/brown hamburger bun

Shaggy Mane
- Edible ☺
- White shaggy cylindrical cap that turns black and inky with age
- Bell shape - mature
- Spore print is black

Death Cap
- Poisonous ☹
- Flattened top
- White cap with brownish scales
- Gills are free and white, turning green as they mature

False Morel
- Poisonous ☹
- Red-brown cap - irregularly lobed, like a brain
- Tube-like hollows
- Yellowish spore print
- Smooth with more wrinkles as it ages

Destroying Angel
- Poisonous ☹
- White stalk and gills
- White cap or white edge and yellowish, pinkish, or tan center
- Egg-shaped cap

Common Conecap
- Poisonous ☹
- Rust-colored brown gills and conical cap
- Surface smooth, dry
- Adnexed gills
- Slender straight stem
- Brown spore print

Deadly Galerina
- Poisonous ☹
- Brownish, sticky cap, yellowish to rusty gills, ring on stalk
- Edges are curved against gills
- Gills narrow, crowded

Lobster Mushroom
- Edible ☺
- Bumpy, reddish-orange exterior
- Fish-like taste
- Irregular shape with little to no stem
- Cracked cap

King Bolete
- Edible ☺
- Light brown to reddish brown
- Stem very thick and club shaped
- White closely spaced small pores
- White flesh

Spore Print

_____
_____
_____
_____
_____

Notes

Location

Site / GPS: _____ Date: _____

○ Living Tree ○ Leaf Litter ○ Mulch ○ Dead Tree or Wood ○ Grass
○ Soil ○ Other _____

Type of Tree(s) On or Near: _____

Forest Type: ○ Deciduous ○ Coniferous ○ Tropical ○ Other _____

Weather Conditions: _____

General

Size (overall height): _____ Color: _____ Spore Color: _____

Texture: ○ Tough ○ Brittle ○ Leathery ○ Woody ○ Soft ○ Slimy
○ Spongy ○ Powdery ○ Waxy ○ Rubbery ○ Watery (Other) _____

Bruising When Touched? ○ Yes ○ No Notes: _____

Structures: ○ Cup ○ Ring ○ Warts _____

Cap Characteristics

Campanulate (bell-shaped)

Conical (triangular)

Cylindrical (shaped like half an egg)

Convex (outwardly rounded)

Flat (with top of uniform height)

Infundibuliform (deeply, depressed, funnel-shaped)

Depressed (with a low central region)

Umbonate (with a central bump or knob)

Surface Markings (warts, scales, slime, etc.): _____

Cap Margin: Smooth, Inrolled, Sinuous/Wavy, Other: _____

Color Changes: _____

Undercap

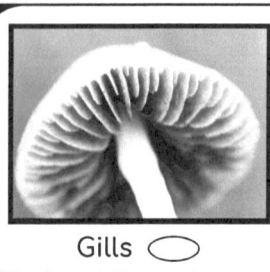

Gills ○
Attachment: Free or Decurrent
Spacing: Crowded, Close, Distant, Subdistant
Color/Bruising: _____

Pores ○
Color: _____
Pore Size: _____
Pore Pattern: _____

Teeth ○
Color: _____
Teeth Length: _____
Flesh: Soft or Tough

Gill Attachment

- **Free** (gills not attached to stem)
- **Adnexed** (gills attached narrowly to stem)
- **Sinuate** (gills smoothly notched and running briefly down stem)
- **Adnate** (gills widely attached widely to stem)
- **Descenting** (gills running down stem for some length)

Stem Shape

- Tapering
- Equal
- Club-Shaped
- Bulbous
- Cup (volva)

Common Mushrooms

Chanterelle
- Edible ☺
- Shape looks like bell of a trumpet
- Bright yellow/orange
- Similar look to Jack o'Lantern

Milk Mushroom
- Edible ☺
- Rounded caps that connect to an elongated, thick stem
- Smooth firm cap
- Color is pure white

Morels
- Edible ☺
- Honeycombed cap
- Most morels cap is longer than stem
- Spore print is usually light colored
- Interior is hollow

Porcini
- Edible ☺
- Large size
- Also known as king bolete
- Resembles reddish/brown hamburger bun

Shaggy Mane
- Edible ☺
- White shaggy cylindrical cap that turns black and inky with age
- Bell shape - mature
- Spore print is black

Death Cap
- Poisonous ☹
- Flattened top
- White cap with brownish scales
- Gills are free and white, turning green as they mature

False Morel
- Poisonous ☹
- Red-brown cap - irregularly lobed, like a brain
- Tube-like hollows
- Yellowish spore print
- Smooth with more wrinkles as it ages

Destroying Angel
- Poisonous ☹
- White stalk and gills
- White cap or white edge and yellowish, pinkish, or tan center
- Egg-shaped cap

Common Conecap
- Poisonous ☹
- Rust-colored brown gills and conical cap
- Surface smooth, dry
- Adnexed gills
- Slender straight stem
- Brown spore print

Deadly Galerina
- Poisonous ☹
- Brownish, sticky cap, yellowish to rusty gills, ring on stalk
- Edges are curved against gills
- Gills narrow, crowded

Lobster Mushroom
- Edible ☺
- Bumpy, reddish-orange exterior
- Fish-like taste
- Irregular shape with little to no stem
- Cracked cap

King Bolete
- Edible ☺
- Light brown to reddish brown
- Stem very thick and club shaped
- White closely spaced small pores
- White flesh

Spore Print

Notes

Location

Site / GPS: _____ Date: _____

○ Living Tree ○ Leaf Litter ○ Mulch ○ Dead Tree or Wood ○ Grass
○ Soil ○ Other _____

Type of Tree(s) On or Near: _____

Forest Type: ○ Deciduous ○ Coniferous ○ Tropical ○ Other _____

Weather Conditions: _____

General

Size (overall height): _____ Color: _____ Spore Color: _____

Texture: ○ Tough ○ Brittle ○ Leathery ○ Woody ○ Soft ○ Slimy
○ Spongy ○ Powdery ○ Waxy ○ Rubbery ○ Watery (Other) _____

Bruising When Touched? ○ Yes ○ No   Notes: _____

Structures: ○ Cup ○ Ring ○ Warts   _____

Cap Characteristics

Campanulate (bell-shaped)

Conical (triangular)

Cylindrical (shaped like half an egg)

Convex (outwardly rounded)

Flat (with top of uniform height)

Infundibuliform (deeply, depressed, funnel-shaped)

Depressed (with a low central region)

Umbonate (with a central bump or knob)

Surface Markings (warts, scales, slime, etc.): _____

Cap Margin: Smooth, Inrolled, Sinuous/Wavy, Other: _____

Color Changes: _____

Undercap

Gills ○
Attachment: Free or Decurrent
Spacing: Crowded, Close, Distant, Subdistant
Color/Bruising: _____

Pores ○
Color: _____
Pore Size: _____
Pore Pattern: _____

Teeth ○
Color: _____
Teeth Length: _____
Flesh: Soft or Tough

Gill Attachment

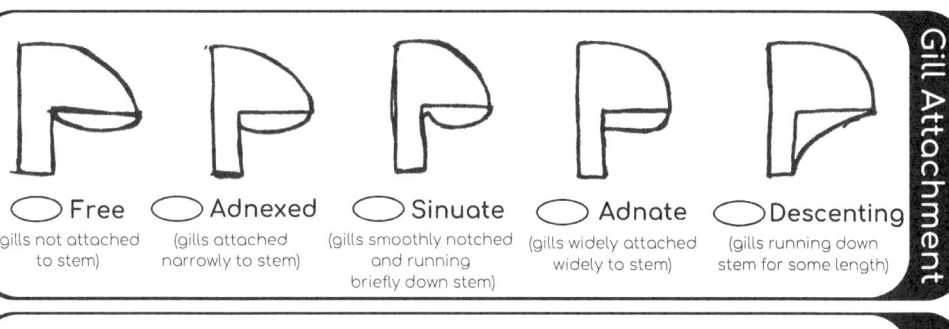

- ○ Free (gills not attached to stem)
- ○ Adnexed (gills attached narrowly to stem)
- ○ Sinuate (gills smoothly notched and running briefly down stem)
- ○ Adnate (gills widely attached widely to stem)
- ○ Descending (gills running down stem for some length)

Stem Shape

- Tapering
- Equal
- Club-Shaped
- Bulbous
- Cup (volva)

Common Mushrooms

Chanterelle
- Edible ☺
- Shape looks like bell of a trumpet
- Bright yellow/orange
- Similar look to Jack o'Lantern

Milk Mushroom
- Edible ☺
- Rounded caps that connect to an elongated, thick stem
- Smooth firm cap
- Color is pure white

Morels
- Edible ☺
- Honeycombed cap
- Most morels cap is longer than stem
- Spore print is usually light colored
- Interior is hollow

Porcini
- Edible ☺
- Large size
- Also known as king bolete
- Resembles reddish/brown hamburger bun

Shaggy Mane
- Edible ☺
- White shaggy cylindrical cap that turns black and inky with age
- Bell shape - mature
- Spore print is black

Death Cap
- Poisonous ☹
- Flattened top
- White cap with brownish scales
- Gills are free and white, turning green as they mature

False Morel
- Poisonous ☹
- Red-brown cap - irregularly lobed, like a brain
- Tube-like hollows
- Yellowish spore print
- Smooth with more wrinkles as it ages

Destroying Angel
- Poisonous ☹
- White stalk and gills
- White cap or white edge and yellowish, pinkish, or tan center
- Egg-shaped cap

Common Conecap
- Poisonous ☹
- Rust-colored brown gills and conical cap
- Surface smooth, dry
- Adnexed gills
- Slender straight stem
- Brown spore print

Deadly Galerina
- Poisonous ☹
- Brownish, sticky cap, yellowish to rusty gills, ring on stalk
- Edges are curved against gills
- Gills narrow, crowded

Lobster Mushroom
- Edible ☺
- Bumpy, reddish-orange exterior
- Fish-like taste
- Irregular shape with little to no stem
- Cracked cap

King Bolete
- Edible ☺
- Light brown to reddish brown
- Stem very thick and club shaped
- White closely spaced small pores
- White flesh

Spore Print

Notes

_____
_____
_____
_____
_____

Location

Site / GPS: _____ Date: _____

○ Living Tree ○ Leaf Litter ○ Mulch ○ Dead Tree or Wood ○ Grass
○ Soil ○ Other _____

Type of Tree(s) On or Near: _____

Forest Type: ○ Deciduous ○ Coniferous ○ Tropical ○ Other _____

Weather Conditions: _____

General

Size (overall height): _____ Color: _____ Spore Color: _____

Texture: ○ Tough ○ Brittle ○ Leathery ○ Woody ○ Soft ○ Slimy
○ Spongy ○ Powdery ○ Waxy ○ Rubbery ○ Watery (Other) _____

Bruising When Touched? ○ Yes ○ No   Notes: _____

Structures: ○ Cup ○ Ring ○ Warts   _____

Cap Characteristics

Campanulate (bell-shaped)
Conical (triangular)
Cylindrical (shaped like half an egg)
Convex (outwardly rounded)

Flat (with top of uniform height)
Infundibuliform (deeply, depressed, funnel-shaped)
Depressed (with a low central region)
Umbonate (with a central bump or knob)

Surface Markings (warts, scales, slime, etc.): _____

Cap Margin: Smooth, Inrolled, Sinuous/Wavy, Other: _____

Color Changes: _____

Undercap

Gills ○
Attachment: Free or Decurrent
Spacing: Crowded, Close, Distant, Subdistant
Color/Bruising: _____

Pores ○
Color: _____
Pore Size: _____
Pore Pattern: _____

Teeth ○
Color: _____
Teeth Length: _____
Flesh: Soft or Tough

Gill Attachment

- **Free** (gills not attached to stem)
- **Adnexed** (gills attached narrowly to stem)
- **Sinuate** (gills smoothly notched and running briefly down stem)
- **Adnate** (gills widely attached widely to stem)
- **Descending** (gills running down stem for some length)

Stem Shape

Tapering, Equal, Club-Shaped, Bulbous, Cup (volva)

Common Mushrooms

Chanterelle
- Edible ☺
- Shape looks like bell of a trumpet
- Bright yellow/orange
- Similar look to Jack o'Lantern

Shaggy Mane
- Edible ☺
- White shaggy cylindrical cap that turns black and inky with age
- Bell shape - mature
- Spore print is black

Common Conecap
- Poisonous ☹
- Rust-colored brown gills and conical cap
- Surface smooth, dry
- Adnexed gills
- Slender straight stem
- Brown spore print

Milk Mushroom
- Edible ☺
- Rounded caps that connect to an elongated, thick stem
- Smooth firm cap
- Color is pure white

Death Cap
- Poisonous ☹
- Flattened top
- White cap with brownish scales
- Gills are free and white, turning green as they mature

Deadly Galerina
- Poisonous ☹
- Brownish, sticky cap, yellowish to rusty gills, ring on stalk
- Edges are curved against gills
- Gills narrow, crowded

Morels
- Edible ☺
- Honeycombed cap
- Most morels cap is longer than stem
- Spore print is usually light colored
- Interior is hollow

False Morel
- Poisonous ☹
- Red-brown cap - irregularly lobed, like a brain
- Tube-like hollows
- Yellowish spore print
- Smooth with more wrinkles as it ages

Lobster Mushroom
- Edible ☺
- Bumpy, reddish-orange exterior
- Fish-like taste
- Irregular shape with little to no stem
- Cracked cap

Porcini
- Edible ☺
- Large size
- Also known as king bolete
- Resembles reddish/brown hamburger bun

Destroying Angel
- Poisonous ☹
- White stalk and gills
- White cap or white edge and yellowish, pinkish, or tan center
- Egg-shaped cap

King Bolete
- Edible ☺
- Light brown to reddish brown
- Stem very thick and club shaped
- White closely spaced small pores
- White flesh

Spore Print

_____
_____
_____
_____
_____

Notes

Made in United States
Troutdale, OR
09/17/2023

12973761R00066